*A*dventure *Guide to*

# The Florida Keys
# & Everglades National Park

## 2nd Edition

## Joyce & Jon Huber

Hunter Publishing, Inc.
300 Raritan Center Parkway
Edison NJ 08818
Tel (908) 225 1900
Fax (908) 417 0482

*in Canada:*
1220 Nicholson Rd.
Newmarket, Ontario
Canada L3Y 7V1
Tel (800) 399-6858
Fax (800) 363-2665

**ISBN 1-55650-745-3**

2nd Edition © 1997 Hunter Publishing

Photo credits:
Page 24 and backcover, Sea World Orlando; 38, 80, 104, 128, 135, 136, 137, 166, 169, Stuart Newman & Associates; 184, courtesy of Amy Slate. All others, Jon Huber.

Maps and illustrations by Joyce Huber.

# Contents

# Preface

The Adventure Guide to the Florida Keys and Everglades National Park is intended to provide details on how and where to enjoy a variety of activities that are often skipped over by ordinary travel guides. We find that most visitors to the region define themselves by what they do. A few confess to just wanting to lie back and do nothing; for them we have a section towards the end of the guide that lists all the great resorts. But the true flavors of this special area can only be tasted by those who venture out of their everyday lives to become scuba divers, snorkelers, canoers, birdwatchers, sea kayakers, deep sea or fly fishermen, swamp hikers and sea sprites. For those of you that fit that description, we've included everything you need to enjoy a variety of outdoor adventures. And to insure future generations some fun, we've added EcoTips, a small collection of earth-friendly ways to leave the area a little better than you found it.

# Acknowledgments

The enthusiasm and assistance of the following people made an invaluable contribution to this guide.

Special thanks to Lissa Dailey, Nikki Krider, and Michael Hunter of Hunter Publishing; Kim Falconer, Stuart Newman Associates; Barbara Fox and Laura B. Quinn, Florida Keys Wild Bird Rescue Center; Larry and Carol Mulvehill; Bob Epstein, Wildwater Productions; Bill Anderson, Old Island Restoration Foundation; David and Cathy Brucas; Ed Carlson, National Audubon Society; Jean, Douglas, and Olver Prew; Dr. Stephen L. Brenner; Camille Mancuso; Josh Neiman, Discover Glassbottom Boat Tours; Barbara Swab and Frank Holler; and Dee Scarr, Touch the Sea.

# Section I

# Planning Your Trip

A unique range of recreational choices combined with a sub-tropical climate attract more than six million visitors to the Florida Keys and Everglades each year. Whatever the outdoor adventurer has in mind, there seems to be a perfect place for it in this part of the world. Activities exist for every age, fitness, and experience level.

Whether you choose to settle in the upper or lower Keys, you are near enough to explore the mysteries and surprises of the other. Everglades National Park main visitor area is a day trip from Key Largo. The Ten Thousand Islands region, favored for fresh-water fishing and canoe camping, is a 95-mile drive from Miami.

## When to Go

The Florida Keys high season has traditionally been from December through May, though many divers and snorkelers prefer the calm and warmer waters of late spring and summer. In winter, skies are predictably sunny and air temperatures range from 75 to 85° F. Fall brings the chance of a hurricane, but offers lower hotel rates and often beautiful weather.

Salt-water fishing is big all year. Comfort-wise, angling the "backcountry" is best in winter, but good fly-fishing in the bays and Gulf of Mexico is more dependent on a full or new moon than the season. This high-tide period occurs twice a month and is published in the tide tables.

Key West attractions are best seen during winter and spring. During summer, though trade winds offer a bit of relief to the other islands, Key West's maze of city buildings blocks the flow, causing uncomfortably hot days during July and August.

Visit Everglades National Park from December through March, the dry season. The rest of the year brings torrential downpours and mosquitoes that cloud the air and cluster in gobs on your skin. We found bugs a problem as late as mid-November, particularly in Flamingo.

# Adventure Tours

Day and half-day sailing, fishing, and snorkeling tours are offered throughout the area. See specialty chapters for listings. Dive shops throughout the US offer group trips covering transportation, diving and accommodations. Snorkelers often may join for a lower rate. Every major resort in the Florida Keys offers a dive-accommodation package, as do many of the Keys dive shops (see Diving and Accommodation chapters for listings).

Money-saving vacation packages for air, hotel and car rental can be arranged through your travel agent. Accommodation-only packages are offered direct from many of the resorts.

Everglades National Park rangers offer guided nature walks and canoe-camping trips.

# Handicap Facilities

Most large resorts feature full handicap facilities. State and national parks have wheelchair-accessible trails, tour boats, accommodations, and restaurants.

The following dive operators offer certification and dives for the handicapped based on "degree of handicap and skill of the diver": **Captain Billy's Key West Diver Inc.**, Stock Island, MM 4.5 (☎ 305-294-7177); **Key West Pro Dive**, 3128 N. Roosevelt Blvd., Key West (☎ 305-296-3823); **Reef Raiders Dive Shop**, 109 Duval St., Key West (☎ 305-294-3635); **Lost Reef Adventures**, Land's End Village, 261 Margaret St. (☎ 305-296-9737); **Looe Key Dive Center**, MM 27, Ramrod Key (☎ 1-800-942-5397 or 305-872-2215); **Strike Zone Charters**, MM 29.5, Big Pine Key (☎ 1-800-654-9560 or 305-872-9863); **John Pennekamp State Park**, Key Largo (☎ 305-451-1202); **Biscayne Aqua-Center**, Convoy Point, Homestead (☎ 305-247-2400) has wheelchair access for their tour, snorkel & dive boats, though no special certifications. **Theater of the Sea**, MM 84.5, Islamorada (☎ 305-664-2431), has wheelchair ramps into the attraction area and the swim-with-the-dolphin pools. For updated information contact the individual resorts and facilities.

# Getting There

All major national and international airlines fly into Miami Airport. Connecting scheduled flights land in Marathon and Key West. No regularly scheduled public transportation exists to Everglades National Park.

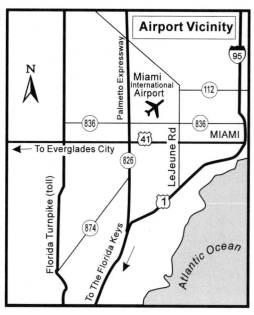

Driving from the North, take Florida Turnpike to Exit 4 – Homestead-Key West. From Tampa, take I-75 south to Naples, then east to Miami and the Turnpike Extension. Or take 41 South, then east to the Turnpike Extension, and finally south to US 1.

## AIRLINES SERVING KEY WEST INTERNATIONAL AIRPORT

| | |
|---|---|
| General flight information | 305-296-5439 |
| American Eagle | 800-433-7300 |
| Cape Air | 305-293-0603 |
| Delta/Comair | 800-354-9822 |
| Gulfstream | 800-992-8532 |
| USAir Express | 800-428-4322 |

## AIRLINES SERVING MARATHON AIRPORT

| | |
|---|---|
| American Eagle | 800-433-7300 |
| Gulfstream | 800-992-8532 |
| USAir Express | 800-428-4322 |

## TO THE FLORIDA KEYS

To reach the Keys from Miami International Airport, take LeJeune Road south to 836 West. Then take the Turnpike Extension to US 1 south, which runs the length of the Florida Keys to Key West.

**Mile Markers** (MM) are used throughout this guide to reference locations in the Florida Keys. They appear on the right shoulder of the road (US 1) as small green signs with white numbers and are posted each mile, beginning with number 126, just south of Florida City. Mile markers end with the zero marker at the corner of Fleming and Whitehead streets in Key West.

Awareness of these markers is useful as Keys' residents use them continually. When asking for directions in the Keys, your answer will likely be at, just before or just beyond a mile marker number.

### TO THE EVERGLADES

**Flamingo.** From Miami Airport, take LeJeune Road south to 836 West, then the Turnpike Extension south to US 1. Turn right off US 1 in Homestead onto State Highway 9336. An 11-mile ride will bring you to the park entrance and the Main Visitor's Center. From there it is a 38-mile trip along the Main Park Road to Flamingo. There are no services along the Main Park Road.

**Everglades City and the Gulf Coast via the Tamiami Trail.** Departing Miami Airport, take LeJeune Road south to 836 West, then Florida's Turnpike south to the Tamiami Trail (Route 41), westbound. Expect a 45-mile ride to Shark Valley and the Miccosukee Indian Reservation. To reach the Gulf Coast Ranger Station, Everglades City and the Ten Thousand Island region, continue an additional 40 miles along Route 41 West to Route 29 South. Then go three more miles to the ranger station. Total distance from Miami to Everglades City averages 95 miles.

### BY BICYCLE

Cyclists are advised to transport their bikes by car from the airport to the Everglades or the Keys. Florida's turnpike does not allow bicycles and US 1, in parts, is devoid of a shoulder and dangerous for road riding. Greyhound will transport your bike to points along US 1 if the bicycle is boxed (see Cycling chapter). Rentals are widely available.

### RENTAL CARS

At **Miami Airport**: Avis, Budget, Hertz, National and Value. If possible, book rental cars in advance of your trip. In season you may be forced to rent more car than you planned.

| Alamo | 1-800-327-9633 or 294-6675 |
| Avis | 1-800-331-1212 or 296-8744 |
| Budget | 1-800-527-0700 or 294-8868 |
| Dollar | 1-800-421-6868 or 296-9921 |
| Hertz | 1-800-654-3131 |
| National | 1-800-328-4567 |
| Value Rent-A-Car | 296-7733 |

## TAXI CABS
### Miami

| Airport Transportation | 453-0100, US 800-749-5397 |
| Checker Cab | 888-8888 |
| Yellow Cab | 444-4444 |
| Diamond Cab | 545-7575 |

### Key Largo - Tavernier

| Sailboat John's | 852-7999 |
| Island Taxi | 664-8181 |
| Airport Trans | 453-0100 |
| A Kokomo Cab | 852-8888 |
| Upper Keys | 453-0100 |

### Marathon

| Island Taxi | 743-0077 |
| Paradise Taxi | 293-3010 |

### Big Pine Key

| Island Taxi | 872-4404 |

### Key West

| Gary's | 289-9840 |
| Maxi Taxi | 294-2222 |
| Pink Cabs | 296-6666 |
| Sun Cab | 296-7777 |
| Yellow Cab | 294-2227 |

### Everglades City Area

| Naples Taxi | 775-0505 |

## TRAINS

| | |
|---|---|
| Amtrak | 1-800-872-7245 |
| Metrorail (Miami) | 638-6700 |

## BUSES

Greyhound buses leave three times daily (7 am, noon and 6 pm) from the airport-vicinity bus station at 4111 N.W. 27th Street, Miami. Travel time to Key West is 4½ hrs. ☎ 800-410-5397, 305-876-7123, or in Key West, 305-296-9072.

The Homestead terminal is at 5 N.E. 3rd Road, Homestead FL 33030. ☎ 305-247-2040.

## BY BOAT

Boaters can reach the area by the inland waterway or outside via the Gulf or Atlantic. The Intracoastal Waterway is limited to shallow draft vessels (5 ft or less). Deep draft boats enroute to Key West follow Hawks Channel, which passes between the outer reefs and the Florida Keys. The Coast Guard Monitors VHF 16.

### Public Boat Ramps

| | |
|---|---|
| Blackwater Sound | MM 110, Bayside |
| Harry Harris Park | MM 92, Oceanside |
| Indian Key Fill | MM 79, Bayside |
| Marathon | MM 54, Bayside |
| West of 7 Mile Bridge | Bayside |
| Spanish Harbour | Bayside |
| Shark Key Fill | Oceanside |
| Cudjoe Key | Bayside |
| Stock Island Ramp | Bayside |
| Key West | end of A1A |

### NOAA Charts

11451 - For small craft traveling from Miami to Marathon & Florida Bay

11465 - Intracoastal Waterway from Miami to Elliott Key

11463 - Intracoastal Waterway from Elliott Key to Islamorada

11462 - Fowey Rocks to Alligator Reef

11452 - Alligator Reef to Sombrero Key

11550 - Fowey Rocks to American Shoal

11449 - Islamorada to Bahia Honda

11448 - Intracoastal Waterway - Big Spanish Channel to Johnson Key
11445 - Intracoastal Waterway from Bahia Honda to Key West
11441 - Key West Harbor & approaches
11447 - Key West Harbor

*Gulf Coast*
11429 - Naples to Pavilion Key
11431 - Pavilion Key to Florida Bay area

## BARE BOATING & CREWED YACHT VACATIONS

Fully-equipped live-aboard motor yachts and sailboats for day trips, overnights or extended vacations, with or without crews can be chartered from the following organizations:

### Atlantic Coast

**Cruzan Yacht Charters,** 3375 Pan American Drive, Coconut Grove FL 33133, ☎ 1-800-628-0785 or 305-858-2822, fax 305-854-0887. Write to: P.O. Box 53, Coconut Grove FL 33133.

Cruzan, operated by Captain Danny Valls, offers a large selection of sail and power bare boats from 30 to 50 ft for half- or full-day, weekend or weekly cruises to Biscayne National Park, the Florida Keys or Bahamas. Day and moonlight cruises may be arranged for two to 12 passengers. Sample rate for a party of six aboard a 50-ft captained sailboat would start at $3,700, plus food, drinks and port taxes. Visa and MasterCard.

**Treasure Harbor Marine, Inc.,** 200 Treasure Harbor Drive, Islamorada FL 33036. ☎ 1-800-FLA-BOAT or 305-852-2458.

Treasure Harbor Marine features day sailboats and live-aboards. High-season prices are from $110 per day for a 19-ft day sail to $330 per day for a 44-ft uncrewed yacht. Rates by the week from $395 to $1,700. Captains available. Lower rates apply between April 1 and November 14th.

**Witt's End.** Captains BJ & Greg Witt offer overnight "bunk & breakfast" outings and weekend or week-long cruises throughout the Florida Keys and Bahamas aboard *Witt's End,* a well-appointed 51-ft ketch docked at Land's End Marina, Key West. Delightful customized, crewed charters include sumptuous breakfasts and candlelight dinners. Sails to prime snorkeling and diving spots. For reservations and prices, write to Captains Witt, P.O. Box 625, Key Largo FL 33037. ☎ 305-451-3354.

## Gulf Coast

**Fort Myers Yacht Charters,** 14341 Port Comfort Road, Fort Myers FL 33908. ☎ 941-466-1800 . Captained, bareboat and lessons.

### PRIVATE PLANE

There are some restrictions for private aircraft flying into the Keys. Light planes must have 12-inch registration numbers and a mode C transponder. A flight plan is required for some areas. Before entering the area, contact the **Aircraft Owner's and Pilot's Association** for a current briefing. ☎ 301-695-2140 or write AOPA Flight Operations Department, 421 Aviation Way, Frederick MD 21701. For water landings, additional information may be available from the **Seaplane Pilot's Association** at ☎ 301-695-2083 or the **Key West Seaplane Base,** ☎ 305-294-6978, fax 305-292-1091. The Miami sectional covers the area.

# What to Bring

### CLOTHING

During winter pack a light jacket, long-sleeved shirts and pants. Temperatures occasionally drop to the 50's. Otherwise, shorts and tee shirts cover most fashion needs, though one change of dressy attire may prove useful.

Scuba divers visiting the Keys between December and March will find a shortie or lightweight wet suit appropriate. Water temperatures drop to the 70's. Winter snorkelers will be most comfortable with a lycra wetskin or light wet suit.

In the Everglades long pants and long-sleeved shirts offer protection from bug bites. Bring sunglasses and a hat that will shade your face.

### GEAR

See individual adventure chapters for details. If you are joining a special interest tour group, avoid mix-ups by labeling all you bring. Colored plastic tape and permanent marker are waterproof. Dive packages often include use of tanks and weights. Bring or plan to rent everything else. Snorkeling equipment is provided by the boat-tour and seaplane operators, but bringing your own insures they fit you comfortably (see Dive and Snorkeling chapters).

*Route 29 cuts through Big Cypress National Park.*

Charter and party boats provide fishing gear. Just bring a cap with a wide brim. The marina stores are well-stocked with tackle and other gear. Polarizing sunglasses such as Cabela's, Corning Serengeti Strata or RayBan are best for spotting fish in the mangrove flats.

Hikers wishing to explore trails off the beaten track should wear submersible shoes. Bring the type with a non-slip sole that won't tear on sharp rocks. Aqua socks or strap-on kayaking sandals are perfect for sloshing around mangrove islands, beach combing and walking on coral rubble.

## SUNDRIES

Mosquito repellent is necessary, especially in summer. Resort areas in the Keys are thoroughly doused with pesticides each evening by a low-flying DC-3 (don't look up when you hear it coming), but state and national parks are considered "natural" and the mosquitoes are left unharmed. One gentle repellent that some find useful is Avon Skin So Soft. Deep Woods Off is more potent and works well against mosquitoes and other stinging insects. Autan, if you can find it, is excellent.

Shopping centers selling everything are scattered throughout the Keys, but off-season (March 15-Nov. 15) campers heading to the Everglades should pack some of everything needed. During winter months the camp store and restaurant at Flamingo are open.

# Credit Cards

With the exception of some small motels, major national and international credit cards are widely accepted throughout the Florida Keys. Money machines are found in the populated areas of the Keys. Personal checks are accepted in some stores with ID – a driver's license and a major credit card. You need a major credit card to rent a car. With rare exceptions, restaurants and stores in Everglades City DO NOT accept credit cards.

# Banks

## MAIN OFFICES

**Barnett Bank,** 1010 Kennedy Drive, Key West, ☎ 292-3860

**First State Bank,** 1201 Simonton St., Key West, ☎ 296-8535

**First Union Bank,** 422 Front St., Key West, ☎ 292-6600

**Nations Bank,** 5401 Overseas Hwy., Marathon, ☎ 743-4121

**TIB Bank,** 994 Overseas Hwy., Key Largo, ☎ 451-4660

## FOREIGN CURRENCY EXCHANGES

**Barnett Bank of the Keys.** All Florida Keys locations: Key Largo, Tavernier, Islamorada, Marathon, Marathon Shores, Summerland Key, Key West.

**First National Bank of the Florida Keys.** All locations: Islamorada, Marathon, Marathon Shores, Key West.

**Kelly's Motel.** MM 104.2, Key Largo. ☎ 305-451-1622 (from foreign to US currency only).

**Citgo Station.** MM 92, Key Largo.

**Key West Currency Exchange.** 1007 Truman Ave., ☎ 305-292-0005.

# Insurance

Standard Blue Cross and Blue Shield policies cover medical costs while traveling. Lost luggage insurance is available at the ticket counter of many airlines. If you have a homeowner's policy, you may already be covered. Some credit cards also cover losses while on vacation. Membership in the American Automobile Association covers unexpected road emergencies for auto travelers.

Inexpensive insurance for rental car mishaps is available from the rental agencies and well worth the price.

Visitors from Great Britain may obtain traveler's coverage from **Europ Assistance**, 252 High St., Croydon, Surrey CRO 1NF, ☎ 01680-1234.

Scuba divers can get health insurance to cover accidents or emergencies that are a direct result of diving for a low annual fee from **Diver's Alert Network** (DAN). A stay in a recompression chamber can cost thousands of dollars and is often not covered by standard medical insurance. For information, stop in your local dive shop or write to DAN, P.O. Box 3823, Duke University Medical Center, Durham NC 27710. ☎ 919-684-2948.

## Helpful Phone Numbers

| | |
|---|---|
| Emergency (Police, Ambulance, Fire) | 911 |
| Florida Highway Patrol | FHP |
| Hospitals | |
| Mariners Hospital, MM 89 | 852-4418 |
| Fisherman's Hospital, MM 48.5 | 743-5533 |
| Florida Keys Health Systems, MM 5 | 294-5531 or 294-5183 |
| Everglades National Park | 305-247-7700 |
| Shark Valley | 305-221-8776 |
| Gulf Coast | 941-695-3311 |
| Biscayne National Park | 305-230-7275 |
| Weather | 305-296-2741 |
| Marine Patrol | 305-743-6542 |
| Coast Guard | 305-743-6388 or 743-6778 |
| Miami area | 305-661-5065 |
| Key West | 305-296-2011 |
| Customs | |
| Miami Area | 305-536-4126 |
| Key West | 305-296-4700 |

# Chambers of Commerce

| | |
|---|---|
| Everglades City | 941-695-3941 |
| | fax 941-695-3172 |
| Key Largo Information | 305-451-1414 |
| | 1-800-822-1088 |
| Islamorada Information | 305-664-4503 |
| Marathon Information | 305-743-5417 |
| Lower Keys Information | 305-872-2411 |
| Key West Information | 305-294-2587 |

**Florida Keys & Key West Visitor's Bureau**, P.O. Box 1147, Key West FL 33041. ☎ US, 1-800-FLA-KEYS; from outside the US, 305-296-3811

**Everglades National Park**, 40001 State Road 9336, Homestead FL 33034. ☎ 305-242-7700

For the **Ten Thousand Islands Region**, contact: Everglades Area Chamber of Commerce, P.O. Box 130, Everglades City FL 33929. ☎ 941-695-3941

# Introduction

Two worlds of beauty welcome visitors to the Florida Keys and Everglades – the only living coral reef system off the continental United States and North America's last remaining wilderness swamp. Together they preserve some of America's most valued and unusual natural resources. So unusual, in fact, that the entire Florida Keys has been designated a National Marine Sanctuary and the Everglades recognized as an International Biosphere Reserve and a World Heritage Site. Overall, the area encompasses five national parks: Everglades, Big Cypress, Biscayne, Dry Tortugas (formally Fort Jefferson National Monument) and the Florida Keys National Marine Sanctuary.

With the exception of Dry Tortugas National Park, which lies 68 miles offshore, you can drive through and see the entire area in two days time. But to really savor this exotic environment it's best to put on your hiking shoes and head for the nature trails, then tour the sea and waterways – go fishing, paddle a canoe, sign up for a glass-bottom boat tour, snorkel or dive the reefs, sail, birdwatch or join an Everglades "slog" (wet hike through water and mud). During summer, mosquitos will bite you no matter what.

# The Florida Keys

Key Largo, the jumping-off point to the Florida Keys, lies 42 miles south-southwest of Miami. The largest of the island chain, Key Largo features John Pennekamp Coral Reef State Park, the first underwater preserve in the United States and the adjacent Key Largo National Marine Sanctuary. Key Largo also boasts the world's only underwater hotel. From Key Largo, the Keys form a southwesterly arc towards Cuba.

All points, from Key Largo to Key West, connect to the mainland and to each other by a cement and steel wonder, The Overseas Highway, a continuation of US Route 1, which follows the roadbed of Henry Flagler's seagoing railroad, built in 1912 but destroyed by an unnamed hurricane in 1935.

This "highway that goes to sea" features 43 bridges and connects Key Largo to Islamorada, and the purple isles – Plantation Key, Windley Key and both Upper Matecumbe and Lower Matecumbe Key. Known as "sportfishing capital of the world," Islamorada, heralded for its angling diversity, features the Keys' largest fleet of offshore charter boats and shallow water "back country" boats.

Marathon Key, the heart of the Florida Keys, houses the local Museum of Natural History and two golf courses. A drive across the Seven Mile Bridge from Marathon leads to the Lower Keys and Key West.

Crossing the Bahia Honda Bridge affords sweeping views of the Straits of Florida and the Gulf of Mexico and brings you to Bahia Honda State Park, with one of the top 10 beaches in the US.

Big Pine Key is noted for the Looe Key National Marine Sanctuary, a spectacular underwater park, and the Key Deer Refuge. Key West, the nation's southernmost city, marks the final stop on the Overseas Highway. Situated closer to Havana than Miami, Key West exerts a charm all its own with quaint, palm-studded streets, century-old gingerbread mansions and a relaxed citizenry of self-styled "Conchs."

Resorts, recreational facilities, restaurants, and shopping areas pave the way from Key Largo to Key West.

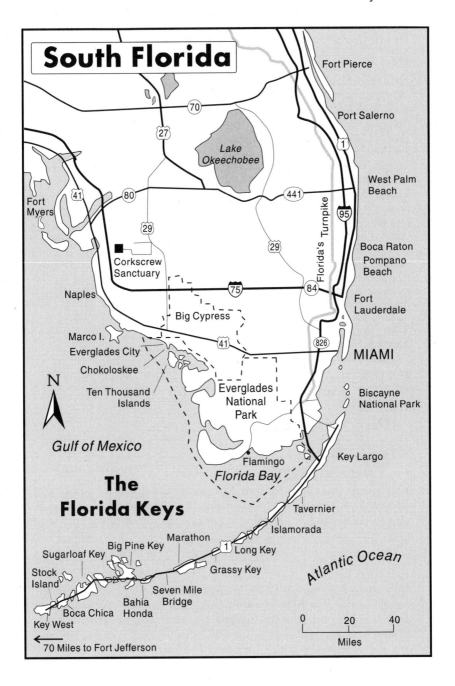

**South Florida**

Fort Pierce

Port Salerno

70

27

*Lake Okeechobee*

West Palm Beach

Fort Myers

41

80

441

Florida's Turnpike

95

29

Boca Raton

29

Pompano Beach

Corkscrew Sanctuary

75

84

Naples

Fort Lauderdale

Big Cypress

41

826

MIAMI

Marco I.
Everglades City

Chokoloskee

Everglades National Park

Biscayne National Park

N

Ten Thousand Islands

*Gulf of Mexico*

Flamingo

Key Largo

**The Florida Keys**

*Florida Bay*

Tavernier

Islamorada

Marathon

1

Long Key

*Atlantic Ocean*

Sugarloaf Key

Big Pine Key

Grassy Key

Stock Island

Seven Mile Bridge

Bahia Honda

Boca Chica

Key West

← 70 Miles to Fort Jefferson

0    20    40

Miles

## Florida Keys National Marine Sanctuary

**Planning Office, 9499 Overseas Hwy, Marathon 33050, ☎ 305-743-2437**

Future generations of visitors may expect to enjoy the continued pristine majesty of the Florida Keys' colorful living reefs, thanks to a 1990 federal law designating the entire Keys island chain as a National Marine Sanctuary. This status allows the designation of reef rejuvenation zones and fish nurseries – areas where diving and fishing are prohibited for select time periods. These sheltered areas allow corals to grow and fish populations to expand. Similar procedures have already proven successful in the Caribbean.

The reefs, which parallel the islands six miles offshore from Key Largo to Key West, attract millions of divers and fishermen annually. In addition to the recreational benefits, the coral reefs protect the islands by forming a critical breakwater that diffuses the energy of storm-driven waves. Plus, the reefs provide sand for Florida's beaches. Scientists estimate that fish nibbling on corals and calcareous algae produce more than 2½ tons of sand per acre annually.

Touring the National Marine Sanctuary rates as one of the Keys' biggest delights. You can view the reefs via dive, snorkel or glass-bottom boat. Expect miles of fish and other reef residents to line up and look you over. They will swim up to your mask and curiously peer back at you through the glass-bottom boat panes. (See Boating, Diving and Snorkeling chapters for details and operator listings.)

## Dry Tortugas National Park

**P.O. Box 6208, Key West FL, ☎ 305-242-7700**

Almost 70 miles west of Key West lie the Dry Tortugas, a cluster of seven uninhabited islands surrounded by healthy coral reefs and renowned for their tropical bird habitats and spring bird migrations. Besides providing a showcase for magnificent wildlife, the islands are the site of Fort Jefferson, America s largest 19th-century coastal fort.

Accessible only by boat or seaplane, the islands feature a visitor center on Garden Key, open daily from 8 am to 5 pm, and safe anchorage in the Tortugas harbor. Contact the park for a list of private carriers. No water, food, fuel, supplies or accommodations are available at the park. Visitors to the park enjoy good fishing, bird watching, snorkeling and self-guided tours of the fort.

Bird checklists are available from the park. (See Aerial and Boat Tour chapters)

Tours of the Fort center around the parade ground, which contains the ghostly remains of two huge buildings – the Officers Quarters and Soldiers Barracks, which were the first structures built at the fort.

# The Everglades

The Everglades region, a great wilderness nurtured by a shallow freshwater river, flows across most of Florida's southern tip. Just six inches deep and 50 miles wide, its riverbed originates at Lake Okeechobee in the north and moves southward. Along its course the riverbed gradually drops 15 feet before emptying into Florida Bay and the Gulf of Mexico. The Indians call it "Pa-hay-okee," the river of grass, for the dense prairies of razor-toothed saw grass that grow in the river. Warmed by the tropical sun, the river breeds algae and insects that nurture fish, turtles and snakes. They, in turn, feed alligators and wading birds. Mounds of higher ground support groves or "hammocks" of hardwood trees, the showcases of the Everglades.

In remote areas, crocodiles share this vast marshland with rare Florida panthers, cougars and the gentle manatee, an aquatic, plant-eating mammal dubbed the "sea cow" for its huge proportions.

Geographically, the Everglades region covers seven million acres south of Lake Okeechobee. Bounded by densely populated resort cities along the east coast and fringed by a maze of mangrove islands that rise from the Gulf of Mexico on its south and western shores, the area encompasses Everglades National Park, Great Cypress National Park, Indian villages along Tamiami Trail, Collier-Seminole State Park, the National Audubon Society's Corkscrew Swamp Sanctuary and the Fakahatchie Preserve.

## Everglades National Park

**40001 State Road 9336, Homestead FL 33034-6733, ☎ 305-242-7700**

Everglades National Park is just a small part of this watery expanse. Established in 1947, the park covers some 1½ million acres. Despite the park's size, its fragile environment is vulnerable to surrounding agriculture, industry and urban development.

During summer, the rainy season, the park presents visitors with a hostile expanse of wet sawgrass prairies, muddy trails and clouds of buzzing insects. But, come the dry period from mid-November through mid-March, the clouds of bugs diminish, as sloughs and

*Snowy egrets browse the Corkscrew Swamp's Wet Prairie.*

trails transform into a welcoming environment for hikers, bird watchers, canoers, and fresh-water fishermen. Alligators and wading birds become easier to spot as they move to deep watering holes near the trails.

Impenetrable mangrove islands, known as the Ten Thousand Islands, web the entire western Gulf shoreline. Between the islands and the mainland exists a flat river, the Wilderness Waterway. Favored for rugged canoe camping expeditions, this shallow water course begins at Everglades City then winds for about 100 miles through shallow creeks and bays to Flamingo, an outpost on Florida Bay, the south tip of Everglades National Park.

## Big Cypress National Park

**HCR 61, Box 11, Ochopee FL 33943, ☎ 941-695-4111**

Some consider Big Cypress National Park the "real Everglades" because it more closely resembles the Hollywood sets. Unlike other National Parks, and despite environmentalists' concern, it is the one area where air-boats, swamp buggies and other off-road vehicles are allowed (by permit). Hunting and trapping continues. It is considered one of the best areas for fresh-water fishing.

A vast swamp more than 1,100 square miles in size, Big Cypress was given park status to protect giant cypress trees from earlier fates as gutters, coffins, stadium seats, pickle barrels and the hulls of PT boats. In 1974, over 570,000 acres were set aside as a National Preserve. In addition to the cypress swamp, the park contains pine islands, wet and dry prairies and mangrove forests. Here, an occasional Florida panther leaves impressive paw marks. Black bears claw crayfish from the sloughs or rip cabbage palmetto apart for its soft fruits.

Eleven thousand acres of Big Cypress are owned by the Audubon Society. Known as the Corkscrew Swamp Sanctuary, this particularly lovely area is a breeding ground for the endangered wood stork.

## Biscayne National Park

**P.O. Box 1369 Homestead FL 33090-1369, ☎ 305-230-PARK**

Biscayne National Park, located 21 miles east of Everglades National Park and six miles east of the Florida Turnpike (Exit #6, Tallahassee Rd.), was designated as a National Monument in 1968. During 1980, it was enlarged and designated as a National Park. Most of it lies underwater. The park boundaries begin below Key Biscayne and encompass the reefs, islands and subsea area from the mainland to 15 miles offshore. The south end abuts the Key Largo National Marine Sanctuary. Biscayne encompasses the uninhabited northern section of Key Largo, Elliot Key, Sands Key, Boca Chita Key and some private islands to the north, the Ragged Keys. The entire area rates high for ocean sports such as canoeing, fishing, diving, snorkeling and wilderness camping.

The Intracoastal Waterway runs through the park boundaries. To reach Biscayne's Convoy Point Visitor Center take either Florida's Turnpike to exit #6, Tallahassee Rd., or travel nine miles east from US 1, Homestead, on SW 328th St.(North Canal Drive). Public boat tours leave from Convoy Point. Anglers and boaters can launch their own boats at the Homestead Bayfront Park boat ramp next to Convoy Point.

# Environment

New environmental buffer zones throughout the Florida Keys and Everglades are being set up to protect and preserve sensitive areas of the ecosystem. In Florida Bay the US Fish and Wildlife Service regulates access to 26 areas of critical concern to wildlife, especially birds and threatened or endangered species. Most areas are small islands. Some are totally restricted; others allow boats to approach by paddle or push pole.

On the ocean reefs, replenishment reserves are being set up to protect and enhance the spawning, nursery or permanent resident areas of fish and other marine life. Some areas restrict fishing and allow diving, but will be "no-take" areas. Prime areas are shallow, heavily used reefs where conflicts occur between different user groups. Special use areas may be established for education, science, restoration, monitoring or research. Currently four areas are being considered: Conch Reef off Tavernier, Looe Key off Big Pine Key, Pelican Shoals and Tennessee Reef off Long Key.

These areas will be continually evaluated, with update cycles modifying or eliminating areas as appropriate.

Jet skis and wave runners may no longer be used in Everglades National Park and Dry Tortugas National Park waters. Studies by the National Park Service and the US Fish & Wildlife Service have indicated that personal water craft users operate their craft in a manner disturbing to wildlife, particularly nesting bird colonies. Most other types of boating activities do not significantly disturb wildlife.

Before diving, fishing, snorkeling, kayaking or boating on your own check with local shops and operators for restricted areas. For additional information write to the **Florida Keys National Marine Sanctuary**, Main House, 5550 Overseas Highway, Marathon FL 33050. ☎ 305-743-2437.

# Water Management

Efficient water management appears to be the first line of defense for Everglades wildlife. In recent years man has realized the enormous impact on national parks and sanctuaries from what happens outside their boundaries.

Weather has a powerful effect on the nutrient levels in Florida Bay and Everglades marshlands. During long dry periods water runoff carrying nutrients and pesticides from dairy and sugar cane farms drains into the canals and wetlands – beginning at Lake Okeechobee then detouring hundreds of miles through residential areas before reaching the Everglades. The chemically treated water eventually reaches Florida Bay and the Gulf of Mexico.

During periods of drought, phosphorus dumped into Lake Okeechobee can raise levels of nitrates and phosphates to 20 times higher than the normally low amounts once found in the sanctuaries. Beneficial algae and oxygen-producing aquatic plants – the spawning ground for fish – are choked out by cattails, which thrive in the phosphate-rich water. On the other hand, periods of heavy rainfall greatly lower the phosphate level and help balance the chemical makeup.

# Algae Blooms

In the ocean and salt-water bays, Florida Bay in particular, an overabundance of nutrients produces algae blooms, which choke out living corals, sponges and turtle grasses. Sponges are the primary habitat for juvenile spiny lobsters, while sea grasses are the primary nursery ground for pink shrimp. Algae blooms have also caused seagrass die-offs on the Atlantic Ocean side of the Keys near the coral reefs.

*Dolphins off Grassy Key.*

At times the algae bloom has covered more than 400 square miles. Sea urchins, which once kept the algae in check, mysteriously died off during 1983. A demand for seafood has caused a large decline in algae-eating fish from over harvesting.

## Additional Recovery Programs

Laws have been passed to return the entire water flow of south Florida to a more natural state. The Dairy Rule of 1987 requires that runoff from pastures be directed into holding ponds. The Surface Water Improvement and Management Act requires pollution reduction and environmental controls by all water management districts. Proposals that huge tracts of farmland be used for pollution filtration are under consideration.

## Parks Play An Important Role

Giving park and marine sanctuary status to larger areas of the region has helped to protect the environment, fund research studies, and educate the public through literature, ranger-led tours and other activities.

*Mangroves, Ten Thousand Islands.*

# The Manatee

The West Indian manatee, a large gray-brown, herbivorous, aquatic mammal found in Florida's shallow coastal waters, canals, rivers and springs, has become a highly endangered species. Population studies indicate that there may be as few as 1,200 manatees left in Florida waters. Many are killed or severely injured by power boats. Habitat destruction puts these docile creatures in jeopardy. Manatees are protected by the Marine Mammal Protection Act of 1972, the Endangered Species Act of 1973 and the Florida Manatee Sanctuary Act of 1978. It is illegal to harass, harm, pursue, hunt, shoot, wound, kill, annoy or molest manatees.

To report manatee deaths, injuries, harassment or radio-tagged manatees, call the **Florida Marine Patrol** at 1-800-DIAL-FMP.

# The Beached-Animal Rescue & Rehabilitation Program

After the Marine Mammal Protection Act of 1972 and the Endangered Species Act of 1973 were passed, marine specialists at Sea World of Florida were approached to aid in the rescue of beached or stranded marine mammals. In cooperation with the Department of the Interior, the National Marine Fisheries Service, the Florida Department of Natural Resources and the Florida Marine Patrol, Sea World developed the Beached Animal Rescue and Rehabilitation Program in 1973. Since that time, animal care specialists have responded to hundreds of calls to aid sick, injured or orphaned manatees, dolphins, whales, otters, sea turtles and a variety of birds.

Sea World bears all costs of the rescue program, including those for research, transportation and rehabilitation. As a result of research conducted by their animal husbandry staff in aviculture, animal care and aquarium departments, valuable baseline data is being established and shared with scientists worldwide. Food preferences, responses to antibiotic therapy, the safest transportation equipment and the swiftest rescue techniques have been documented by the staff. This data is invaluable in the effort to protect marine mammals from extinction. Sea World is the largest of the two facilities in the state that are authorized to rescue, care for and release manatees.

## Seabird Sanctuary

The Florida Keys Wild Bird Rehabilitation Center in Tavernier offers visitors a close encounter with recuperating pelicans, spoonbills, hawks, herons, owls and ospreys. Many of the injured and orphaned birds can be patched and returned to the wild to live on their own. Executive Director Laura Quinn and center volunteers are licensed by the Florida Fish and Game Commission and are members of the National Wildlife Rehabilitators Association. The rehabilitators work in conjunction with local veterinary clinics to aid birds with eye, neck, chest, wing and leg injuries.

The center's educational efforts include information on handling injured birds and techniques for removing fishing lures and hooks. (see Fishing chapter "Eco Tip" for details)

## Dolphin Sanctuaries

Injured or ailing dolphins and those stressed out from performing in circuses and attractions are finding rest and retirement care at the Grassy Key Research Center, Theatre of the Sea, Islamorada and holding pens that are being set up in the Keys.

*Grunts frequent reefs throughout the Keys.*

# Reef Relief

Many factors, both natural and those caused by human intrusion, contribute to the destruction of a coral reef. Some relief has been gained by the mooring buoy system, one of the most effective programs to reduce anchor damage and to provide you with a convenient means of securing your boat in the sanctuary. The buoys are available on a first-come, first-served basis for everyone.

# Turtle Hospital

Richie Moretti and partner Tina Brown operate the first turtle hospital in what used to be an exotic dance lounge next to Moretti's motel, Hidden Harbor Motel in Marathon.

The turtle hospital has complete surgical facilities, including a sterilized operating room, pre- and post-operative care and a research room. An apartment for a live-in veterinarian is situated above the hospital.

The endangered green turtle, *chelonia mydas*, named for its greenish color, can weigh up to 330 pounds and is characterized by a pair of scales on the front of its head, a white or yellowish bottom shell and paddle-shaped flippers with one claw.

Half the green sea turtle population is suffering from the plague called fibropapilloma, a mysterious disfiguring disease that causes tumors to grow internally and on the fleshy parts of the turtle's eyes, mouth, neck, flippers, jaw and tail. The tumors get so big that they blind the turtle, and the sick turtles eventually starve or drown.

Currently, researchers associate the tumors with a type of herpes virus. Moretti and Brown are working with University of Florida veterinarian Elliot Jacobson to pinpoint the cause and find a cure for fibropapilloma.

Jacobson's research and travel to and from Marathon are supported in part by the Keys organization of Save the Turtles. One modification Moretti has done to his property to assist with the research is convert one of the motel swimming pools into a saltwater holding area for ailing turtles. Guests of Hidden Harbor can observe the ongoing research efforts and are often recruited to assist the staff.

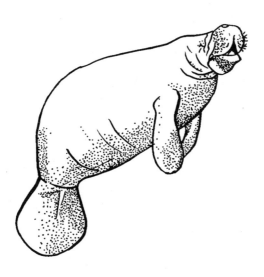

# History

Not long after Christopher Columbus discovered the New World in 1492, adventurer Ponce de Leon and fellow Spanish chronicler Antonio de Herrera sighted the Florida Keys. That was Easter Sunday, May 15, 1513.

Herrera wrote for posterity: "To all this line of islands and rock islets they gave the name of Los Martires because the rocks as they rose to view appeared like men who were suffering; and the name remained fitting because of the many that have been lost there since."

The name Florida was later chosen from the Spanish name for Easter: Pascuas Florida.

Florida remained under Spanish rule until 1763 when the British captured Havana and traded it for Florida. By 1783 it was back under Spanish rule. In 1818, under President Thomas Jefferson's leadership, the US bought Florida for five million dollars.

## The Indians

The Calusa and Tekesta Indians first populated the southern Everglades and the Keys. To the north were the Seminoles and Miccosukees. Word of Bahaman natives being carried from their homeland and forced into slavery by the white man prepared the Calusas to defend their freedom fiercely. Early attempts by the Spaniards to settle in the Keys were met with the sting of arrows. In 1521, a band of Calusas in primitive canoes attacked approaching Spaniards. Among those struck down was Ponce de Leon when an arrow pierced his suit of armor. He later died in Havana. Wars between the Indians and the white man raged on for centuries. Many of the original Indian tribes died off from white man's diseases, some were taken into slavery by the Spaniards and moved to Cuba and other areas of the Caribbean.

Many runaway black slaves sought refuge in the Everglades and were taken in by the Indians. This, along with border disputes, fueled the Indian battles with the US.

By 1817 US troops led by Andrew Jackson forced most of the Indians to reservations in the West. But, one tribe, the Seminoles, never surrendered to US forces. Indian attacks on the Keys continued into the mid-1880's.

Descendants of the Seminoles and the Miccosukees still populate the Everglades region. Both tribes migrated from Georgian Creek tribes during the early 1700's in search of better fishing, hunting and farm lands. They found all three in the Everglades.

Shallow off-shore oyster beds provided the Indians with an easy food source. The cast-off shells grew into huge mounds, which today attract interest as archaeological finds and are protected in Everglades National Park as historic preserves. Mound researchers have uncovered ancient tools, pottery, animal and human bones.

On the other hand, Chokoloskee Island, a huge shell mound in the northwest Everglades region, has been paved over and made into an RV camp.

## Pirates

In the years following Ponce de Leon's first sighting, many Spanish and British vessels cruising the Florida straits became targets of piracy – first by the Indians, later by notorious figures like Henry Morgan, Blackbeard, Gasparilla, Black Caesar, and Lafitte. The pirates' small boats easily outmaneuvered and outran the huge pursuing Navy frigates. By 1821, attacks on US shipping became common and continued until 1823, when the US government dispatched Commodore David Porter. He swiftly replaced the large frigates with small schooners and one old ferry boat. Finally able to negotiate the shallows, Porter's men put a fast end to piracy.

# Forts

After Florida became part of the United States in 1821, military officials recognized the strategic importance of the Dry Tortugas. The nation that occupied the islands would control navigation in the Gulf.

Fort Jefferson – the "Gibraltar of the Gulf" – was built on Garden Key in the mid-1800s and lies among a cluster of seven coral islands called the Dry Tortugas. The fort walls measure eight feet thick and rise to 50 feet high. It has three gun tiers designed to hold 450 guns.

The fort was never fired upon, but during the Civil War it served as a military prison for captured deserters. For almost 10 years after the fighting stopped, it remained a prison. Among the prisoners sent here in 1865 were four of the so-called "Lincoln conspirators" – Michael O'Loughlin, Sammuel Arnold, Edward Spangler, and Dr. Samuel Mudd – who had been tried and convicted of complicity in the assassination of Abraham Lincoln. The most famous of these was Dr. Mudd, a Maryland physician who, knowing nothing of Lincoln's murder, had set the broken leg of the fugitive assassin, John Wilkes Booth. Sentenced to life imprisonment, Mudd was pardoned in 1869 for helping to fight the 1867 yellow fever epidemic that struck the fort, felling 270 of the 300-man garrison and resulting in 38 fatalities.

The cell occupied by Dr. Mudd during his years of confinement can still be seen at the fort today.

It took 21 years of hard labor, hurricanes and yellow fever epidemics – from 1854 to 1866 – to build the trapezoid-shaped Fort Zachary Taylor on Key West. During the Civil War, the Union controlled the fort on the island with strong local support. Fort Taylor was the home base for a successful blockade of Confederate ships, and some historians say the blockade cut a year off the War between the States. Two more Key West forts, East and West Martello Towers, were authorized by Congress in 1844 to protect Fort Taylor from enemy attack, but neither was ever completed. Fort Taylor is believed to hold the largest number of Civil War artifacts in the nation and has become a major archaeological treasure.

# Wrecking & Sponging

The absence of lighthouses and reliable charts made early ocean travel hazardous in the shallow waters surrounding the Florida Keys. During storms many ships crashed on the reefs and became prey to wreckers, who often killed all aboard for possible treasure.

By the 1830's law and order prevailed and a more civilized type of salvaging came into play. Upon sighting foundering ships, the wreckers sailed out, saved the passengers and cargo in return for 25% of the haul. Wrecking became Key West's most profitable industry, though some say the ships were still deliberately lured on the shoals. Non-farming settlers in Key West and at Islamorada became wreckers and Key West became the wealthiest city in the infant United States Republic from the bounty of that profitable industry. By 1886, improved charts, the advent of steam-powered ships, and the construction of lighthouses and lighted marker towers on the reefs put an end to the wrecking business. Carysfort Light, off Key Largo, was the first of the navigational beacons.

Sponge farming and exporting soon replaced the Key West wrecking industry. By the turn of the century Key West grossed $750,000 yearly in sales. Sponging continued till 1904 when overharvesting depleted the supply. Greek spongers were blamed. Unlike Keys spongers, who harvested by reaching down with long hooked poles, the Greeks dove on the sponge beds wearing weighted metal boots and diving helmets, enabling them to gather more sponges. Local workers claimed the Greek's heavy boots were destroying the sponge seeds and ruining the gardens. The industry moved to Tarpon Springs where it thrived until 1938 when a blight dried up Florida's days as a sponge port.

# Farming & Shark Skins

In 1822 Key West became the Keys' first permanent settlement. Spaniards who first set foot on the island found it littered with piles of bones and thus named it Island of Bones or Cayo Hueso – a

*Cigar maker Raul Castro (right) at the Southern Cross Club, Key West.*

name that later became Anglicized into Key West. Early settlers farmed productive groves of Key limes, tamarind and breadfruit. In the lower Keys, pineapple farms flourished, producing up to one million crates a year. Besides fresh fruit sales, a Keys processing factory shipped canned pineapple to most of Eastern North America. As air transportation and refrigeration improved, Hawaiian plantations eventually took over the pineapple market.

In later years, a thriving shark factory was established on Big Pine Key amidst the abandoned farms. It employed workers to catch sharks and skin the hides, which were then salted down and sent north to a factory in New Jersey where they were processed into a tough leather called shagreen, an abrasive skin used by cabinet makers for sandpaper.

# Plume Hunting

In the 1870's women's fashion dictated the use of enormous feathers in their hats. Plume hunting grew to huge proportions in the Everglades. Greedy hunters ravaged the nesting grounds of egrets and herons, killing thousands of birds to sell to the millinery trade. Desperate to stop the slaughter, the Audubon Society sent game wardens to protect the rookeries. Finally, the public took notice when newspapers covered the death of Guy Bradley, a game warden murdered by the plume hunters. By 1890 the bird population was badly depleted, but national publicity about the murder raised public concern and brought an end to plume hunting.

## Cigars

During the mid-1800's Cuban cigar makers established factories in Key West. By 1880, 166 cigar factories produced over 100 million cigars per year. But once again, Key West's golden days were numbered. Continuing labor disputes forced the cigar industry to Tampa. It was also in 1880 that talk began of draining the Everglades for farmland.

## The Spanish-American War

Key West took on historic importance when its harbor served as a port to warships during the Spanish-American War. Though Tampa was the principal base for military activity, the Key West Navy Yard, just 90 miles from Havana, became a jump-off point for hospital and supply ships. At a special memorial in the Key West cemetery rest the bodies of those who died when the US battleship *Maine* was sunk in Havana's Harbor in 1898, the event that touched off the Spanish-American War.

## Flagler's Railroad

In 1903, railroad tycoon Henry Flagler built his impossible railroad "that went to sea," transporting wealthy visitors to vacations in the Florida Keys. The railroad extended rail service from Homestead to Key West and to Cuba by sea-going ferries that carried the cars across the Gulf. On Labor Day in 1935, a nameless hurricane ravaged the keys with 200-mph winds and an 18-ft tidal surge. It ripped out the huge caissons that had been constructed to connect

*The* Maine *Monument, Key West*

the islands. Though most of the bridges held up, the rail beds on the lowlands were destroyed. They were never rebuilt. Sections of the old railroad bridges remain and can be seen in the lower Keys.

In the depression years the Keys faced a bleak future. The city of Key West went bankrupt.

It was then, with Federal aid, that Keys officials decided they still had something to offer – sea, sun and a good winter climate. In this somewhat weather-beaten, shabbily genteel setting of the 1930s, the idea of a highway to replace the railroad was born. The famed Florida Keys Overseas Highway (US 1) opened in 1938. Three years later World War II dashed all the prospects of tourist gold.

The US Navy came to the rescue again to build a submarine base in Key West. Shrimp were discovered – the Keys' now vital pink gold – and, following the war, the tourists finally began to come in earnest.

## The Tamiami Trail

The western Everglades region remained largely unexplored until 1915 when construction of the Tamiami Trail began. Workmen were plagued by mosquitoes, and snakes. Many deaths resulted from snakebites and related fungus infections. Armed guards were eventually hired to shoot the snakes. A good portion of the road-bed was built on wet mud, which often caused the heavy machinery to sink or fall over. Completion seemed impossible. Work crews endured despite the hardships and the 120-mile road linking Miami to Tampa was dedicated on April 26, 1928. With the completion of the Tamiami Trail and, in 1938, the first overseas highway from the mainland to Key West, commercialization of the area began. Tourism and land development have since boomed.

# Section II

## Outdoor Adventures

## Aerial Tours

If light plane tours are a new addition to your adventure list, be sure to book an early-morning flight on a day with calm winds. Rising columns of air that cause light aircraft to bounce are more prevalent as afternoon sun heats the ground. Winds, if gusting, may also cause a bumpy ride. Don't forget to bring binoculars and a camera.

Most sightseeing tours skirt the Atlantic side of the islands, where intriguing panoramas of sun, sand and sea await. As you climb out, the view stretches to an azure horizon dotted with sparkling white dive and fishing boats. Dolphin sightings are frequent and on clear days you can easily pick out individual snorkelers and swimmers.

Or, if you choose sightseeing over the Everglades wilderness, you'll enjoy breathtaking views of vast marshlands and the varied plant communities that thrive there.

Crossing the Everglades at low altitude, you may spot the silhouette of a manatee or a huge alligator beneath the water's surface. West of Everglades City in the Ten Thousand Island region, narrow waterways twist and turn into a mosaic of exotic shapes.

## Everglades

**Wyatt Aviation Service** at Homestead General Aviation Airport offers aerial tours of Everglades and Biscayne National Parks. ☎ 305-247-7757

*Fort Jefferson, now a National Monument, can be visited by boat or charter seaplane service from Key West.*

## The Keys

Private light-plane sightseeing tours to any point in the Keys are offered at the **Cessna Pilot Center**, Marathon Airport. ☎ 305-743-4222.

## By Seaplane

Foremost in out-island tour popularity are half-day seaplane excursions to Fort Jefferson in the Dry Tortugas. Located 70 miles west of Key West, the fort is the most inaccessible National Monument in the Western Hemisphere. The islands, off the beaten path, were named for their lack of fresh water and once-abundant turtle population. Today, prime attractions are the spectacular snorkeling found on the surrounding coral reefs and a chance to explore the historic hexagonal brick fort where Dr. Samuel Mudd was imprisoned for his alleged part in the assassination of President Lincoln.

On the flight out you'll spot numerous shipwrecks and the treasure site of Spanish galleons, *Atocha* and *Margarita*. When the sea is calm the clear waters of the Gulf magnify an outline of the wrecks. Flights can be booked through the Key West Seaplane Base for a morning or afternoon departure.

There are rest rooms on the island, but no food or beverage service facilities. You must bring everything with you. And, while plans to add a picnic lunch or possibly a beach barbecue to the seaplane itinerary are in the works, at this writing passengers are advised to pack their own snacks and cold beverages. The flight time ranges from 30 to 40 minutes. The planes, float-equipped Cessnas, carry up to five passengers. Cost is presently $159 per person (price may fluctuate).

Key West Seaplane Base, located on Stock Island, operates year round. Turn right onto Junior College Road from the southbound lane of Route 1. The turnoff is just before the bridge to Key West. A sign on Junior College Road directs you left behind the golf course to the base. For reservations, ☎ 305-294-6978; fax 305-294-4660. All flights are weather-dependent and take place only during daylight hours. Free snorkeling gear is available.

### ABOUT FORT JEFFERSON

Situated on Garden Key, the immense 50-ft-high fort was once considered a strategic point for controlling navigation through the Gulf. Construction of the brick and stone fort was started in 1846 and, although work continued for almost 30 years, little was done after 1866. Updated weaponry introduced during the war, particularly the rifled cannon, had made the fort obsolete.

Then in 1864 engineers discovered that the fort's foundations rested not upon a solid coral reef as originally thought, but upon sand and coral boulders washed up by the sea. As the huge structure settled, the eight-ft-thick walls began to crack. Though never a target of military action, the fort served as a prison for Civil War deserters and periodically as an anchorage for the American naval fleet. The Army abandoned the fort in 1874 following a damaging hurricane and an outbreak of yellow fever. In 1935, President Franklin D. Roosevelt rescued the fort from oblivion and proclaimed the area a National Monument.

# By Open Cockpit

For a romantic tour of Old Key West, hop into the front seat of an open-cockpit biplane. Bring a friend; it seats two. The pilot rides in the back. Helmets and goggles supplied.

Fred Cabanas, chief pilot and owner of **Island Aeroplane Tours**, offers a wide range of scenic flights. Choose a ride over south-shore beaches and island resorts; or a view of Mallory Square and Old Town Key West; an island shipwreck excursion, which takes you over Channel West of Fleming Key; or combine them all with a coral-reef tour. Fred's "See-it-All" tour starts by flying over a visual maze of coral reefs, then heads west to Boca Grand Island

(13 miles west of Key West), over Woman Key, Man Key and Ballast Key. The over-ocean flights offer excellent photo opportunities. Passengers often spot sharks, rays and migrating schools of fish. Rates vary depending on air time and are apt to fluctuate. All flights depart Key West International Airport. Island Aeroplane Tours is just off South Roosevelt Boulevard at Key West Airport. ☎ 305-294-TOUR (8687) for reservations.

## Aerobatic Flights

If flying over the ocean in an antique biplane isn't adventure enough, tighten your leather helmet and goggles for the ultimate – an aerobatic ride in a Pitts S-2A. You've always wanted to be a stunt pilot and do a loop? Great! Strap yourself in and take a lesson. For a moment the ocean becomes the sky, and the sky the sea below. Do this before lunch.

Reticent companions can relax in knowing the aerobatic flights are single-passenger only. And instructor-pilot Fred Cabanas flies 3,500 passengers a year, holds an Air Transport rating and is currently training his 13-year-old daughter Kelly to fly the Pitts. Also at Island Aeroplane Tours. ☎ 305-294-TOUR.

## For the Traditionalist

Flights in a standard, high-wing, four-seat Cessna are offered by **Island City Flying Service** at Key West International Airport. While these flights may not provide quite the romance and adventure of water flying or barnstorming in an open cockpit, the view is still splendid and the price tag a bit lower; in the front seat you can open the window and take pictures. Aim straight down to keep the wing strut out of the shot. You can also arrange for a night flight over the city. Rates start at $60. Flying lessons are offered too. For reservations, ☎ 305-296-5422.

# Boat Tours

## Royal Tours Aboard The *African Queen*

Half-hour cruises on the *African Queen* depart from the Holiday Inn docks (MM 100). Powered by the original engine, the *Queen* lets off steam as the first mate sounds the fog horn and pulls away from the dock. The ride lasts about a half-hour.

Occasionally, owner James Hendricks joins the tour and passes around his photo journal. It includes notes to Hendricks from Katherine Hepburn, foreign dignitaries, and photos from his European, Canadian, Australian and US tours. Upon return, passengers are given honorary *African Queen* captain licenses and a postcard of her for remembrance. Hendricks, dubbed the "jovial millionaire" by southern journalists, is indeed aglow as he shares his prized possession with guests. He purchased the vessel in 1982 and restored her to the original condition.

The *Queen*, a coal-powered steam boat, was built in Lytham, England in 1912 for service in Africa on the Victoria Nile and Lake Albert, where the movie was filmed in 1951. She was used by the British East Africa Railway from 1912 to 1968 to shuttle cargo and passengers across Lake Albert, located on the border between the Belgian Congo and Uganda.

Stop by the Key Largo Holiday Inn Resort to view the *Queen* or call to reserve a seat, ☎ 305-451-4655.

*Key West's amphibious "Duck" splashing down at Land's End Marina.*

## Key West Ducks

Tour Key West by land, then splash down into the sea aboard an antique DUKW military amphibious vessel. The tour lasts 70 minutes, most of it at sea, and includes a narration on the unique history and oddities of Key West. Board the Duck at 1111 Eaton Street, behind Two Friend's Patio Restaurant in the heart of Old Town. ☎ 305-296-7001.

## Mangrove Tours

Caribbean Watersports at the Sheraton Key Largo Resort (MM 97) offers "Enviro-Tours" on your choice of a shallow-draft Zodiac inflatable or a Hobie Cat sailboat. Tours take off across Florida Bay, with a flexible itinerary that varies according to the winds and tides. Most float past uninhabited islands and through mangrove creeks. On any given outing you may come upon endangered species like the Florida manatee or the American bald eagle, pods of bottle-nosed dolphins or you may have a shark encounter with baby blacktips or bonnetheads while they skim the shallows for food. Sign up at the beach shack at the Sheraton or ☎ 800-223-6728; in Key Largo, 852-4707.

# Airboats

Originally designed for hunting, airboats are now used for sight-seeing the sawgrass prairies and mangrove thickets along the Tamiami Trail and Everglades City. Sign up for an exhilarating ride at any one of the following operators: **Wootens** (☎ 941-695-2781), **Bill & Ed's Excellent Airboat Adventures** (☎ 941-695-4959), **Everglades Private Airboat Tours** (☎ 941-695-4637), **Jungle Erv's Airboat Tours** (☎ 941-2805), **Swampland Airboat Tours** (☎ 941-695-2740), or **Speedy Johnson's Fun Cruise** (☎ 941-695-4448).

Nearer to Miami, also on 41, you can arrange for a ride at the **Miccosukee Indian Village,** ☎ 305-223-8388 weekends, 305-223-8380 weekdays. Most airboat sightseeing trips last 30 minutes. Airboats are not allowed within Everglades National Park boundaries. The noise frightens wildlife and disrupts nesting grounds.

# Everglades National Park Tours

Scenic boat tours through the Ten Thousand Islands region are arranged at the Everglades National Park, Gulf Ranger Station on Chokoloskee Causeway. The 2½-hour, ranger-guided trip stops briefly for shelling on Kingston Key, a small island on the edge of the Gulf. Frequent sightings of porpoise, manatees, eagles, nesting ospreys, and roseate spoonbills are reported. Schedules of departure times and prices are posted at the concession office and on the bulletin board at the Gulf Coast Ranger Station. ☎ 941-695-2591 for reservations and additional information. Or write to Everglades National Park Boat Tours, P.O. Box 119, Everglades City FL 33929.

# Tours Departing Flamingo

Similar tours through Florida Bay depart the Flamingo marina. ☎ 305-242-7700 or write to Everglades National Park, 40001 State Rte 9336, Homestead FL 33034.

# Fort Jefferson & The Dry Tortugas

Tortugas Ferry operates *Yankee Freedom*, a luxurious, 100-ft high-speed cruiser that departs Land's End Marina, Key West for day tours of the Dry Tortugas. The yacht averages 25 knots per hour, with travel time from Key West to the Tortugas approximately

 **SAVE A MARINE CREATURE**

Each year more than 100,000 marine animals die from eating or becoming entangled in plastic debris. Sea turtles, whales, dolphins, manatees, fish and sea birds mistake plastic bags and balloons for jellyfish. Swallowing a plastic bag or balloon has caused many of these animals a slow and painful death by blocking their digestive tracts, thus starving them to death.

Sea birds' bills and heads have gotten twisted up in the plastic rings from six packs of beer and soda cans.

You can help prevent these mishaps by disposing of all your trash properly and discouraging others from throwing trash overboard.

Never release a helium-filled balloon in the air. Pick up any discarded fishing line you see around docks and marinas. Plastic six pack rings should be cut up before placement in the recycling bin.

---

three hours and 15 minutes. Amenities include air-conditioned cabin, spacious sundeck, complete galley, complimentary breakfast, full bar.

Day tours offer an opportunity to explore Fort Jefferson, swim, snorkel the beautiful reefs surrounding Garden Key, birdwatch and beachcomb.

The ferry leaves Key West at 8 am and returns at 7 pm every Monday, Wednesday, Friday and Saturday. Current price is $75, with some discounts for seniors, kids, and groups. ☎ 305-294-7009 or 800-634-0939. Trips are weather-dependent and will be cancelled when winds exceed 25 knots. Rates and schedules are subject to change.

## Glass-Bottom Boat Tours

Glass-bottom boat tours are entertaining and educational. They offer a long look at the living reefs that parallel the Florida Keys from Key Biscayne to Key West. Most boats have rest rooms, a snack bar and operate throughout the year. **Biscayne National**

*The African Queen.*

**Underwater Park, Inc.** operates a 53-ft glass-bottom boat in Biscayne National Park, a coral reef area that stretches from the southern tip of Key Biscayne to the northern tip of Key Largo. As boats pass over the shallow reefs, visitors get a look at submerged WWII aircraft wrecks inhabited by huge nurse sharks, angel fish, turtles, spiny lobster, parrot fish and schools of grunts and sergeant majors. The boats depart Convoy Point. Be sure to phone ahead to confirm schedule. Most days trips depart at 10 am and 1:30 pm. ☎ 305-247-2400.

In Key Largo, one especially good trip is aboard the *San Jose* at John Pennekamp State Park. The two-hour excursion brings you eight miles out to Molasses Reef, an area favored by divers for its mazes of coral canyons and fish life. The boat's seating area for the above-water portion of the tour is quite high and enables you to view nesting cormorants eye-to-eye at the channel markers. It also allows for a fine aerial view of winding cuts and trails laced into the mangroves as a narrator points out nesting spots for osprey, herons, kingfishers or roseate spoonbills. After passing through the mangrove channels of South Sound Creek to your left, you can see mud flats, which are a feeding area for hundreds of wading birds. The birds are attracted by the edible debris and silt that collects on the shallow bar. Once on the reef, the boat slows down and you move down into the viewing salon. This area varies from boat to boat.

As the boat slithers through the coral canyons that form the reef, you are inches away from swaying lavender seafans, walls of curious grunts, and angel fish. A fierce-looking barracuda may come up and look back at you as you pass through a profusion of bubbles. As the boat glides through mazes of antler, staghorn and brain corals the narrator points out mating wrasses, neon parrot-fish and other curious reef residents.

Crew members of the *San Jose* tell us that the two things passengers ask to see are sharks and turtles. Sharks are a rare sight on the Pennekamp reefs, but turtles are seen on half of the trips. Queen and French angels, barracuda, parrotfish, wrasses, schools of grunts, and moray eels are more commonly seen. Groups may book a private tour through John Pennekamp Park, on which you first see the reef through the viewing salon, then move to a shallow reef for snorkeling. ☎ 305-451-1621. Or write to **Coral Reef Park Co.**, P.O. Box 1560, Key Largo FL 33037.

Similar Pennekamp Park tours are offered aboard the *Key Largo Princess*, a 70-ft glass-bottom aluminum motor yacht. It carries 125 passengers and is tied down at the Holiday Inn Docks, MM 100, Key Largo FL. ☎ 305-451-4655.

The *San Jose* and the *Key Largo Princess* both have air-conditioned salons – especially desirable during summer months.

In Key West, glass-bottom trips aboard the *Discovery* leave from the foot of Margaret St. at the Half Shell Raw Bar. The tour is two hours. The narration combines the colorful waterfront history of Key West and points of interest on the living coral reef. Call ahead to book a sunset or day cruise on the *Discovery*. ☎ 305-293-0099. Glass-bottom/snorkeling excursions off Key West are offered by **Lange's Coral Princess** fleet, located at the end of Front Street. There are two trips daily, all gear and instruction included. ☎ 305-296-3287. Note: If you are prone to motion sickness, take preventative measures before leaving the dock. The slow rocking motion of the boats crossing the reefs causes most mal-de-mer.

## Sunset Tours

In Key Largo, sunset tours depart the Quay Beach Club (MM 102) and Caribbean Watersports at the Key Largo Sheraton (MM 97), ☎ 305-852-4707, nightly. Bay cruises visit Bird Island, home to many pelicans, herons and ibis. Bring binoculars.

Former park ranger Chick Charney offers Everglades birdwatch tours departing Key Largo, ☎ 451-8393.

Sail off into the sunset on one of Key West's own tall ships, the Schooner *Liberty*, the Schooner *Wolf* or the Windjammer *Appledore*.

*The Wolf*, a 74-ft two-masted schooner, departs the Key West Bight Marina at the foot of William Street for daily snorkel trips and romantic sunset cruises. ☎ 305-296-WOLF (9653). The *Liberty* sails from Hilton Resort & Marina at Front & Greene Streets. ☎ 292-0332. Windjammer *Appledore* cruises depart the foot of William Street. ☎ 296-9992. Catamaran sunset-sail cruises are through **Fury Catamaran** (☎ 294-8899), **Sebago Catamarans** (☎ 294-5687), **Sunny Days Catamaran** and **Stars & Stripes Catamarans** (☎ 294-7877).

Book two-hour sunset dance cruises aboard the motor yacht *Moon Dancer*. Amenities include two full-service bars, dance floors, and a snack bar. ☎ 294-0990.

## Liveaboards & Bare Boating

Groups as small as six can charter a 50-ft sailing yacht for a week, complete with captain and cook, for under $1,000 per person. Trips are custom-suited to your group for diving, snorkeling or simply relaxing. If you are an experienced sailor or boater, you can charter a 30-ft or larger sail or motor yacht starting from about $1,000 for seven days.

**Cruzan Yacht Charters**, 3375 Pan American Drive, Coconut Grove FL 33133, ☎ 800-628-0785 or 305-858-2822, fax 305-854-0887. Cruzan offers a large selection of sail and power bare boats from 30 to 50 ft for full- or half-day, weekend or weekly cruises to Biscayne National Park, the Florida Keys or Bahamas. Sample week rate for six aboard a 50-ft captained sailboat would start at $3,700, plus food, drinks and port taxes. Visa and MasterCard.

**Treasure Harbor Marine, Inc.** 200 Treasure Harbor Drive Islamorada FL 33036, ☎ 1-800-FLA-BOAT, 305-852-2458. Treasure Harbor Marine offers day sailboats and live-aboards. Prices range from $110 per day for a 19-ft day sail to $330 for a 44-ft uncrewed live-aboard. By the week from $395 to $1,700. Crews available.

*Witt's End*. Captains BJ and Greg Witt offer "bunk & breakfast" outings for overnight, weekend or week-long cruises throughout the Florida Keys and Bahamas aboard *Witt's End*, a well-appointed 51-ft ketch docked at Land's End Marina, Key West. Delightful customized, crewed charters include sumptuous breakfast and candlelight dinners. Sails to prime dive and snorkeling spots. For reservations and prices write to Captains Witt, P.O. Box 625, Key Largo FL 33037. ☎ 305-451-3354.

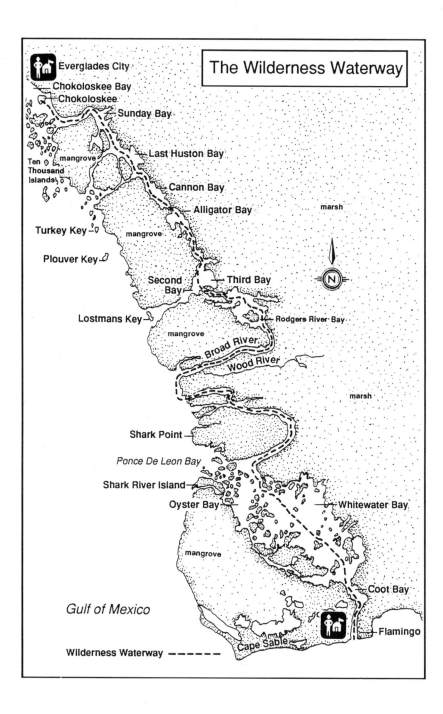

The Wilderness Waterway

Everglades City
Chokoloskee Bay
Chokoloskee
Sunday Bay
Last Huston Bay
Ten Thousand Islands
mangrove
Cannon Bay
Alligator Bay
marsh
Turkey Key
mangrove
Plouver Key
Second Bay — Third Bay
Lostmans Key
mangrove
Rodgers River Bay
Broad River
Wood River
marsh
Shark Point
Ponce De Leon Bay
Shark River Island
Oyster Bay — Whitewater Bay
mangrove
Coot Bay
Gulf of Mexico
Cape Sable
Flamingo
Wilderness Waterway — — — — —

# Canoe & Kayak Tours

Canoe and kayak tours offer close encounters with Florida's exotic birds and fish, dolphins, manatees and alligators. Sea kayaks are favored for snorkeling and ocean outings, while canoes are the choice for backcountry creeks, streams and mangrove trails. Both permit access to shallow-water wilderness areas where other boats can't go. In fact, powerboats are prohibited on many mangrove trails.

Paddling tours can be short or long range, guided or self-guided and as adventurous as you want. Prices start at $25 for short tours and from $100 per day for week-long trips. The marked trails in Florida's Keys (from Key Largo to Key West) are recommended for beginners. If you are new to paddling, ask the canoe or kayak renter to give you a short lesson and demonstration in paddling skills and safety. Ultimately, you must determine your own skill level and plan your adventure accordingly. Biscayne National Aquatic Park, just south of Miami, offers easy canoeing in unpopulated waters. Winds and tides are the most important factors in planning your paddling tour. Tides can create strong currents. First-time canoe or kayak renters should stick to short protected trails. Let someone on shore know where you're going and how long you expect to be out. Don't overestimate your abilities or underestimate the elements. Begin all your trips into the wind, allowing an easier trip home.

## The Florida Keys

A three-mile wilderness canoe trail at John Pennekamp State Park offers calm waters and well-marked routes. Located on Key Largo at MM 102.5, this spot makes an excellent choice for beginners. The trail, sheltered by dense walls of mangrove, offers a look at sea birds, an array of tropical fish and an occasional manatee. Off-limits to powerboats, it makes a tranquil setting for a morning or afternoon paddling adventure.

You may encounter some current, but it is usually very light. The park has changing facilities, rest rooms, fast food counter, gift shop, two beaches, shaded picnic and camping areas.

Wildlife photography opportunities abound. Brown pelicans glide gracefully overhead as cormorants dive and great white herons stalk the shore for food fish. Ducks will swim right up to your craft and flying fish may surprise you by skimming the surface along-side your bow. In winter, the lovely pink roseate spoonbill may appear in the mangrove shrubs along the trail. Crystal clear water allows a good look at French and queen angelfish, barracuda, parrot fish and an occasional turtle.

Weather permitting, rentals and guided canoe trips are available. Canoes and tikis (small kayaks) rent for a low hourly rate. You must be at least 18 years old in Florida to sign for a rental. Write to **Coral Reef Park Co.**, P.O. Box 1560, Key Largo FL 33037. ☎ 305-451-1621.

**Florida Bay Outfitters** (next to the Caribbean Club, Key Largo, MM 104) offers kayak and canoe rentals, camping equipment, and guided tours on Florida Bay. Free Keys chart with rental. Write to Florida Bay Outfitters, 104050 Overseas Hwy., Key Largo FL 33037. ☎ 305-451-3018.

In Islamorada, **Papa Joe's Marina** (MM 79.7) offers single and double kayaks for rent on an hourly basis, seven days a week. ☎ 305-664-5505. Further down the Keys, **Ocean Paddle South** (2244 Overseas Highway, Marathon) gives eager kayakers several options: single or double kayaks for a 24-hour period from the store location, or by the hour and half-day from beautiful Bahia Honda State Park.

Protected trails along the shallow flats of Long Key State Recreational Area (MM 67.5) wind through dense mangrove swamps, home to a huge wading-bird and marine life population. In fact, the island was once home to the Long Key Fishing Club, a mecca for the world's greatest saltwater fishermen until its destruction by a hurricane in 1935.

During the winter months, park rangers offer programs on the ecology of the area. Canoe rentals available. Write **Long Key State Recreation Area**, P.O. Box 776, Long Key FL 33001. ☎ 305-664-4815.

Relaxing guided wildlife tours to and around the mangrove islands off Key West are offered by **Mosquito Coast Kayaks**, 1107 Duval St., Key West FL. ☎ 305-294-7178. Trips start at 8:45 am and return at 3:00 pm. Cost $45.

Mosquito's experienced back-country guides lead you through the shallow mangrove channels and fringe reef areas while explaining the natural history of the area. Tour events vary. You may chase a four-foot nurse shark or a sting ray through the shallows or meet up with a bald eagle. Tropical fish, sea turtles and hundreds of other species of water animals are visible below the surface, along with shore plants, algae, sea grasses, sponge and corals.

Your guide will also teach you how to get in and out of your kayak, so you can snorkel and explore a small secluded coral reef, or show you how to sail in a 15 mph wind with a large kite.

Key West kayak tours are also offered by **Adventure Charters**, 6810 Front St., Stock Island, ☎ 305-296-0362, and **Blue Water Tours**, ☎ 800-331-1771.

In the lower Keys, **Reflections Kayak Nature Tours** promotes excursions into the Great White Heron National Wildlife Refuge and surrounding mangrove islands. Write to P.O. Box 430861, Big Pine Key. ☎ 305-872-2896.

**Lost World Adventures** provides four-hour guided tours into the islands of the Great White Heron Refuge, the Key Deer Refuge and the Coupon Bight Aquatic Preserve. Write to P.O. Box 431311, Big Pine Key. ☎ 305-872-1040.

Select from a two-hour trip to Pelican Island, a unique seabird habitat, backcountry tours, or ocean tours to secluded beaches where you can snorkel, picnic and beachcomb. Tours include use of a stable, lightweight one- or two-person kayak and transportation to and from the departure location. The sea kayaks are longer and wider than whitewater kayaks and rudder controls are available. A double kayak measures more than 18 feet long. Spray skirts are not used, allowing the occupants to remain cool and comfortable.

Biscayne National Park, a new area popular for canoeing, covers 181,500 acres of pristine mangrove shorelines, islands, bays and offshore coral reefs.

Shallow-water routes follow the southern shores of Biscayne Bay near park headquarters (US Rte 1 & SW 328th St.). Canoes are rented by the park concessionaire next to the Visitor Center. For additional information, write to **Biscayne National Underwater Park**, P.O. Box 1270, Homestead FL 33090. ☎ 305-230-1100

# Everglades National Park Canoe Tours

Everglades National Park is a much more rugged environment for canoeing and kayaking than the Florida Keys, but perfect for those who want a true wilderness adventure. Here experienced canoe and kayak enthusiasts com-

*Florida alligator.*

bine paddling with superb fly fishing and backcountry camping.

If you are new to canoe and kayak paddling, this is not the place to learn on your own. Gain experience by joining a guided tour group. The presence of alligators, crocodiles and murky water makes swimming and wading, by intent or accident, undesirable. Seasonal low water and high mosquito levels can ruin even a short trip. Before going out on long trails you must be competent at marine navigation, and have a working knowledge of weather patterns, tides and currents in the area. The season is from early November through the end of April. Summer storms and a ferocious mosquito population take over the park from May through October.

Before embarking on any Everglades paddling tours be sure to file a float plan 24 hours in advance with the park rangers and ask for a current trail condition report. This will advise you of current water and mosquito levels. Pre-trip advisories are crucial, especially during dry winter months when water levels in spots may drop to less than an inch, leaving you in waist-deep mud.

There is an inland water route from Everglades City on the Gulf of Mexico to Flamingo on Florida Bay. Sequentially numbered markers guide you over its 99 miles. Known as the **Wilderness Waterway** (see maps below), the route twists through expansive marine and estuarine areas of the park. These areas harbor almost every type of marine organism found in the Caribbean and serve as spawning grounds and nurseries for many of them. Larger creatures such as water birds, sea turtles, many types of fish sought by fishermen, and the endangered manatee are attracted to these waters because of their abundant food supplies. The route requires a minimum of seven days by canoe and a small motor is recommended.

Primitive campsites are available along the route. Backcountry camping permits are required and may be obtained from the Everglades City or Flamingo ranger station. The permits are issued daily between 7:30 am and 4:00 pm. Charts 11430, 11432 and 11433 cover the area and are for sale at the main Visitor Center, Flamingo and in the Everglades City area.

Give plenty of space to power boats. In shallow areas they may not be able to come off a plane without hitting bottom. Stay to the right and turn your bow into their wake.

# Canoe Camping

If you are canoe camping, carry at least one gallon of water per person per day. There is no fresh water in the backcountry. And be certain to bring trash bags. You must pack all your trash out with you. Food and water must be packed in hard shell containers. Raccoons will chew through plastic jugs and styrofoam coolers. Pets are not allowed in the backcountry or on the canoe trails. Finding dry firewood is difficult. Bring a portable stove using compressed gas or liquid fuel.

Mosquitoes and sand fleas can be overwhelming, particularly after a rainstorm. You'll need an ample supply of insect repellent and a tent with fine mesh screening. We found Deep Woods Off repellent effective, but in extreme wet periods you are better off heading away from the marsh lands completely. The bug problem cannot be overemphasized. Veteran canoe camper Joe Van Putten describes the mosquitoes' arrival as follows: "You don't see them, you hear them coming. At first, I thought it was airplanes."

# Map 1

### Wilderness Waterway
### Chokoloskee Bay to Sunday Bay

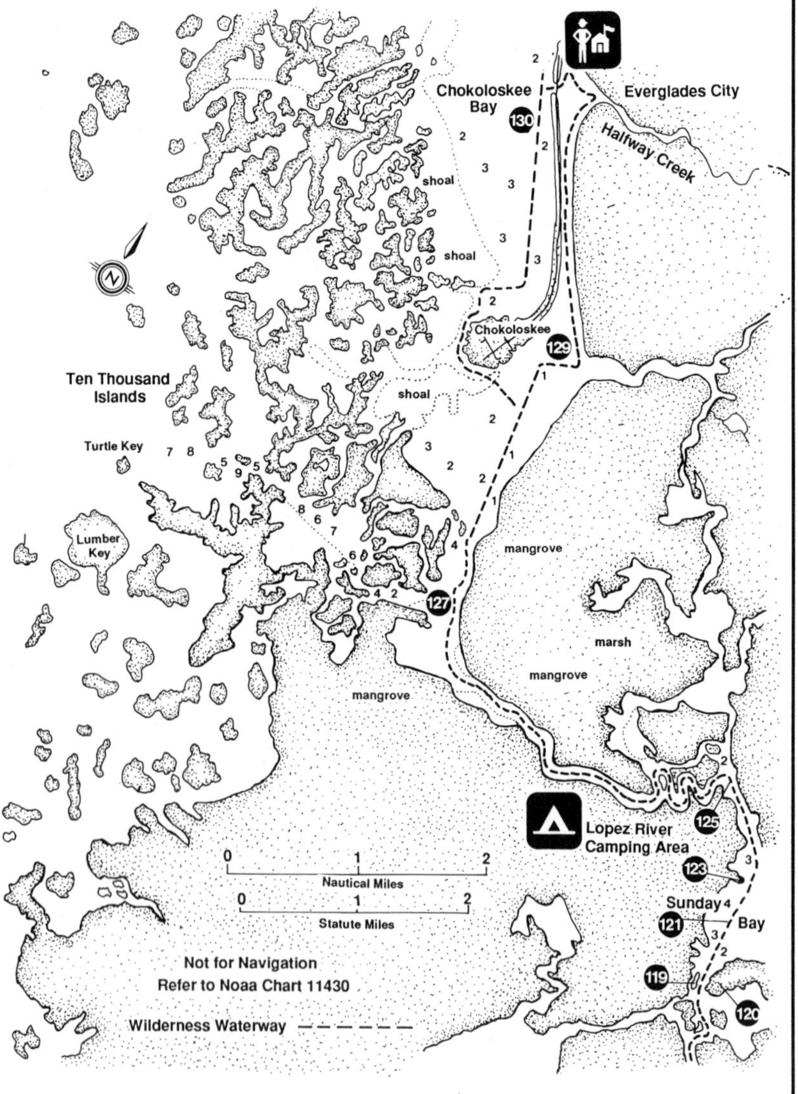

Chokoloskee
Bay

Everglades City

Halfway Creek

130

2

2

shoal

3

3

3

3

2

Chokoloskee

129

1

Ten Thousand
Islands

shoal

2

Turtle Key

7  8

5

9  5

3

2

2

1

1

8

6
7

mangrove

6
4

4

marsh

4  2

127

mangrove

mangrove

mangrove

2

Lumber
Key

Lopez River
Camping Area

125

123

3

Sunday

4

121

3

Bay

2

119

120

0              1              2
Nautical Miles

0              1              2
Statute Miles

Not for Navigation
Refer to Noaa Chart 11430

Wilderness Waterway  — — — — —

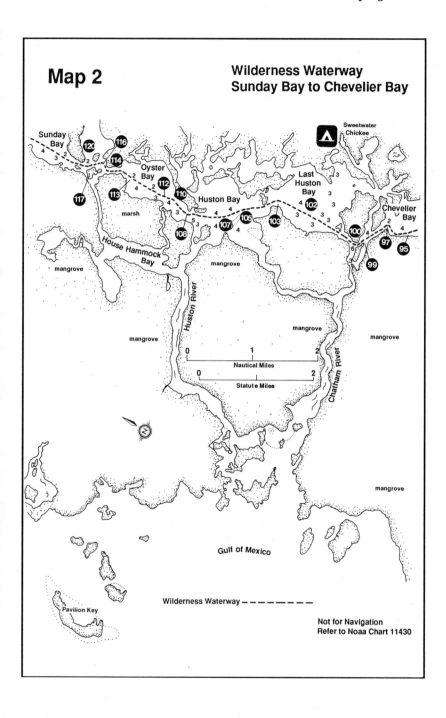

# Map 2

**Wilderness Waterway
Sunday Bay to Chevelier Bay**

Sunday
Bay

Oyster
Bay

Last
Huston
Bay

Sweetwater
Chickee

Chevelier
Bay

Huston Bay

House Hammock Bay

marsh

mangrove

mangrove

mangrove

Huston River

Chatham River

mangrove

mangrove

mangrove

0        1        2
Nautical Miles

0        2
Statute Miles

Gulf of Mexico

Pavilion Key

Wilderness Waterway  — — — — — —

Not for Navigation
Refer to Noaa Chart 11430

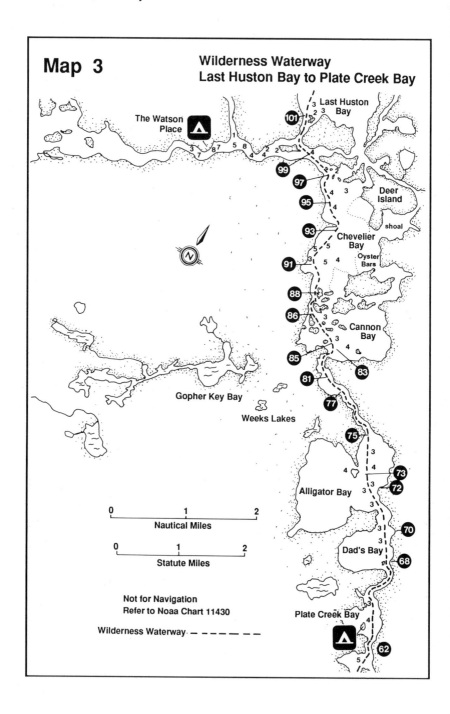

Map 3

Wilderness Waterway
Last Huston Bay to Plate Creek Bay

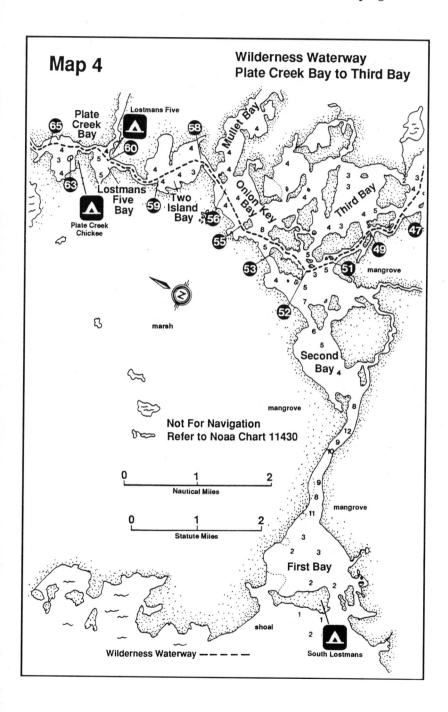

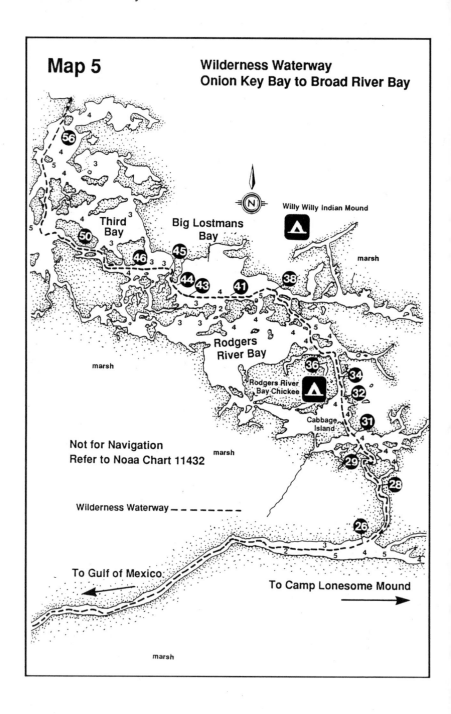

# Map 5

**Wilderness Waterway
Onion Key Bay to Broad River Bay**

56

Third
Bay

50

46    45

44 43    41    38

Big Lostmans
Bay

N

Willy Willy Indian Mound

marsh

Rodgers
River Bay

36    34

Rodgers River
Bay Chickee    32

Cabbage
Island    31

29

Not for Navigation
Refer to Noaa Chart 11432

marsh

28

Wilderness Waterway — — — — — — —

26

To Gulf of Mexico

To Camp Lonesome Mound

marsh

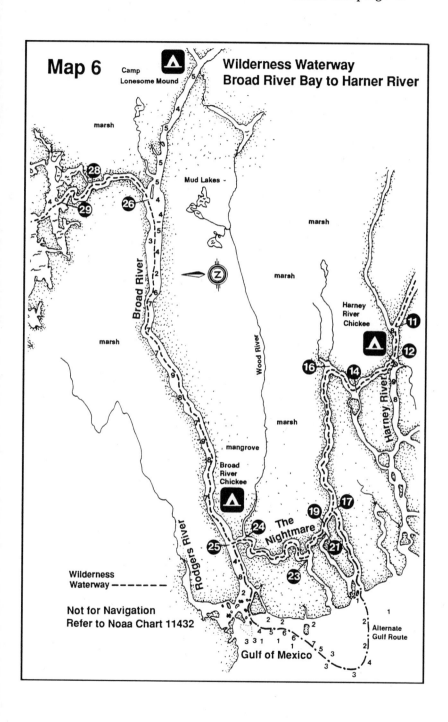

**Map 6**

Camp Lonesome Mound

**Wilderness Waterway**
**Broad River Bay to Harner River**

marsh

Mud Lakes

28

29  26

Broad River

marsh

N

marsh

Wood River

marsh

mangrove

Broad River Chickee

Rodgers River

Wilderness Waterway ———

Not for Navigation
Refer to Noaa Chart 11432

Harney River Chickee

16  14

11

12

Harney River

17

19

24  The Nightmare

25  21

23

Gulf of Mexico

Alternate Gulf Route

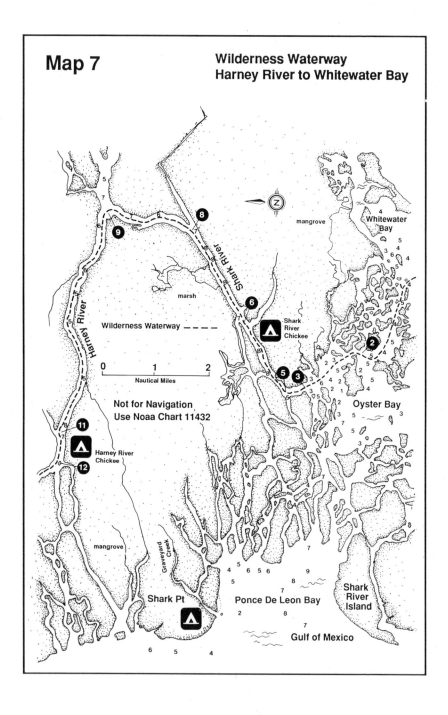

# Map 7

## Wilderness Waterway
## Harney River to Whitewater Bay

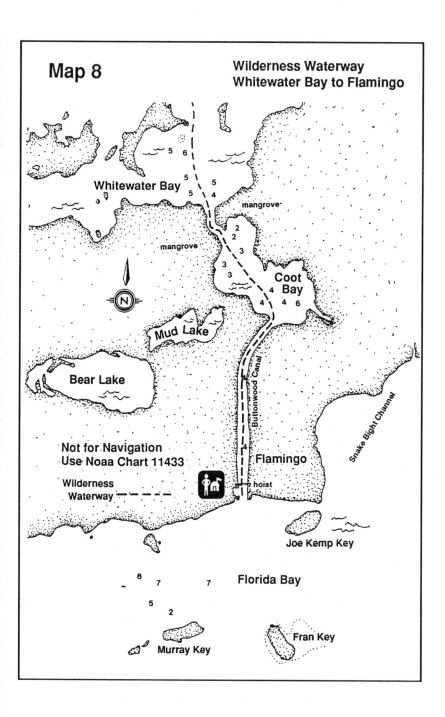

**Map 8**

Wilderness Waterway
Whitewater Bay to Flamingo

5   6

Whitewater Bay
5
5
5
4

mangrove

2
2
3

mangrove

3
3

Coot
Bay

4
4   4   6

N

Mud Lake

Bear Lake

Buttonwood Canal

Snake Bight Channel

Not for Navigation
Use Noaa Chart 11433

Flamingo

Wilderness
Waterway

hoist

Joe Kemp Key

6
7        7        Florida Bay

5
2

Murray Key

Fran Key

 **HELP SAVE A BROWN PELICAN**

Do not feed pelicans large fish carcasses that they cannot easily swallow. The bones from these large fish will kill them.

Properly dispose of fishhooks, fishing line, six-pack rings, plastic bags and other trash.

Encourage others to recycle and pick up cans and bottles in the water, on the beach or along the roadside.

See Fishing chapter for wild bird rescue tips.

## Ten Thousand Islands Day Trips

Trips within the Ten Thousand Island sector originate on Chokoloskee Bay at Everglades City. You can rent a canoe at the **Everglades National Park Boat Tours** office or at **North American Canoe Tours** across the street, at **Outdoor Resorts** on Chokoloskee Island, or bring your own. Put in at the canoe ramp next to the Ranger Station or next to Outdoor Resorts on Chokoloskee Island.

Don't panic if you tip over. Chokoloskee Bay is shallow; it may be possible to walk to land. Be sure to have keys and valuables where they will not be lost in the water. Time your trip so the tides help you. A falling tide flows toward the Gulf of Mexico, a rising tide flows toward the Ranger Station. If you have questions about handling a canoe, ask a ranger for assistance.

## Sandfly Island Trip

Follow the marked channel south. Optional: circle the island in shallow water – you may have to walk your canoe across the oyster bar north of the island. Watch for strong tidal currents south of the island. The dock on Sandfly Island is two miles from the Ranger Station. There is a nature trail on Sandfly Island that features natural and cultural history. Estimated paddling time: 2½ hours.

## Chokoloskee Bay Loop

Follow the marked channel west, then south; turn east and follow the north margin of the Ten Thousand Islands to the other marked channel; turn north and follow the marked channel back to the

Ranger Station. This trip is mostly open water with a few small mangrove islands not dependable for landing, especially at high tide. Estimated paddling time: 2½ hours.

## Collier Seminole State Park

Collier Seminole State Park is at Route 92 and the Tamiami Trail, about 17 miles west of Carnestown – the turn-off for Everglades City. A limited number of visitors are allowed to visit this preserve each day by canoe. A 13½-mile canoe trip through a buttonwood and white mangrove forest, then through a salt marsh, will offer a look at several of the state's endangered and threatened species. These include wood storks, bald eagles, red cockaded woodpeckers, crocodiles, manatees, Florida black bears, Florida panthers and mangrove fox squirrels. Tent and RV camping, saltwater fishing, and canoe rentals are available. Write Collier Seminole State Park, Rt. 4, Box 848, Naples FL 33961. ☎ 813-394-3397.

## Flamingo Area Canoe Trails

**Nine Mile Pond.** This scenic, 5.2-mile loop trail starts at the Nine Mile Pond parking lot and takes approximately four hours. The trail, well marked with white plastic posts, crosses an open pond and curls through freshwater prairie, sawgrass and mangrove habitat. Watch for alligators, wading birds and an occasional snail kite. The course may be difficult to follow, but during summer months it is the preferred trail as it is relatively insect-free. During the winter dry season, portions may be impassable due to low water levels. No motors permitted.

**Noble Hammock Trail** begins between Nine Mile Pond and the Hells Bay trailhead on the east side of the main park road. It passes through open country and small alligator ponds, through buttonwood, red mangrove and sawgrass. Its sharp corners and narrow passes require good maneuvering skills.

Historically, the trail was used for access into some of the larger hammocks for bootlegging operations and many of the old cuttings to mark the trail can still be seen. Traveling this three-mile loop takes three hours. Check for low water levels during the dry season. No motors permitted.

**Hell's Bay** trailhead sits half-way between Nine Mile Pond and West Lake on the west side of the main park road. Named by old timers because it is "Hell to get into and Hell to get out of," this sheltered route weaves through mangrove-lined creeks and ponds to a series of small bays beyond the Lard Can campsite. The trail may be difficult to follow – keep an eye out for markers. The first campsite lies approximately four miles from the starting point or within three hours travel time. The second campsite is in Hell's Bay and lies four miles from the first site, or 4½ hours travel time.

This trail gives the best opportunity to travel through overgrown passageways of red mangrove and brackish water environment. Be sure to check the water levels before starting the journey. Use of motors is prohibited from trailhead to the Lard Can campsite, but a 5½ hp motor may be used elsewhere on the trail. A Backcountry Use Permit is recommended when traveling this trail, even when not camping.

**West Lake Trail**, an eight-mile, seven-hour tour, begins at the West Lake interpretive shelter and winds through a series of large open lakes connected by narrow creeks lined with mangroves. Alligators and crocodiles are numerous.

Large, exposed areas along this route require extra caution on windy days. The trail meanders between thickets of red and black mangrove and buttonwood trees, then through the remains of a once-great forest destroyed by hurricanes. Redfish and sea trout abound. A small clearing for primitive camping exists at Alligator Creek. Park rules prohibit the use of any motor from the east end of West Lake to Garfield Bight.

**Buttonwood Canal**, a three-mile trail leading to Coot Bay, offers a look at alligators, crocodiles and birds. Several power boats use this route and should be given the right of way.

**Mud Lake Loop,** connecting the Buttonwood Canal, Coot Bay, Mud Lake and running along the Bear Lake Canoe Trail, shelters a variety of habitats and wildlife. Motors are prohibited. Starting 4.8 miles from the Bear Lake trailhead, Mud Lake Loop is accessible from the Flamingo Marina through Buttonwood Canal or the Bear Lake Trailhead.

## OBEY RESTRICTED ACCESS SIGNS

Stay a minimum distance of 100 yards from bird roosting, nesting and feeding areas. If your presence appears to be flushing birds from their activities, you are too close and should move farther away

*Roosting ibis.*

**Bear Lake Canal**, an 11½-mile route, leads to Cape Sable's Camping Area, the last wilderness beach left in south Florida. To get there, you paddle along a narrow, shady canal. Accessible from the Flamingo Marina through Buttonwood Canal with a portage from the Bear Lake trailhead. Impassable between markers 13 and 17 during the dry season (January through April). Motors prohibited.

Consult NOAA nautical chart 11433 for the location of shoal water (sand bars, mud banks, shallows).

Tides can create strong currents. Low tides at East Cape are at least two hours earlier than Flamingo low tides; high tides at East Cape are 1½ hours earlier than Flamingo high tides.

## Safety Equipment Checklist

____ Flotation Gear. Florida law requires a Coast Guard-approved personal flotation device for each occupant.

____ First Aid Kit. Add insect repellent and sunscreen.

____ Extra paddle.

____ Bow and stern lines.

____ Flashlight and extra batteries.

____ Compass.

____ Charts.

For additional information, write to Everglades National Park, 40001 State Road 9336, Homestead FL 33034-6733. ☎ 305-242-7700.

# Everglades Canoe Rentals

**Flamingo Lodge Marina & Outpost Resort**. Flamingo FL 33030. ☎ 305-253-2241 or 914-695-3101.

**Biscayne National Underwater Park, Inc.**, P.O. Box 1270, Homestead FL 33030. ☎ 305-230-1100.

**Everglades National Park Boat Tours**, P.O. Box 119, Everglades City FL 33929. ☎ 914-695-2591 or 800-445-7724 (Florida only).

# Canoe Outfitters

Canoe outfitters offer all-inclusive guided trips, which may include pick-up from the airport, transportation between sites, tents, canoes, and meals. All you are required to bring is yourself and a change of clothing. Rates start at $100 per day. Groups are usually small – 10-12 people. Singles and couples mix. You can bring your own group or join one formed by the outfitter. You must book in advance.

**Mountain Workshop, Inc.** of Ridgefield CT offers full blown adventure-travel expeditions through Everglades National Park and Florida's Keys, including canoeing, airboating, diving, snorkeling, parasailing, hiking and more. Special nature education programs are available for school groups, youngsters (11-15) and biology study groups. Tours are from November through April (listing below). Mountain Workshop, Inc. (group tours only), Corky Clark, P.O. Box 625, Ridgefield CT 06877. ☎ 203-438-3640.

**Hawk, I'm Your Sister**, of Santa Fe, New Mexico, offers one annual Everglades canoe tour for women only and one for couples of any configuration.

**North American Canoe Tours** offers guided and "you-paddle" tours, which can be a half-day to a week or longer. They provide everything you need: a 17-ft all-aluminum Grumman canoe, personal flotation devices, paddles for two, a photocopy of local maps, a cooler with ice and drinking water. They also run a low-cost, 10-room bed and breakfast inn, The Ivey House, at Everglades City (listing below). North American Canoe Tours, Inc., D. Harraden (winter address), P.O. Box 5038, Everglades City FL 33929. ☎ 941-695-4666; (summer address), 65 Black Pt. Rd., Niantic CT 06357. ☎ 203-739-0791.

## APPROACH SEAGRASS BEDS GENTLY

Seagrass beds provide nursery areas, feeding habitat and shelter for a wide variety of marine animals. Alert and knowledgeable boaters can help protect this precious resource.

Accidental groundings and turbidity from boat wakes destroy seagrass beds. Recovery may take as long as 10 years.

Use navigation charts and make sure you have adequate water depth to avoid scraping the flats. Color changes in the water indicate differences in depth and bottom types. Shallow seagrass beds, hard-bottom, patch reefs and sand shoals in near-shore areas will appear beige, brown or light green. Deeper adjacent waters are darker green. Wearing polarized sunglasses greatly enhances subtle differences in water color.

# Canoe Trip Equipment Check List

_____ Flotation device(s)

_____ Paddles

_____ Bailer

_____ Bow and stern lines

_____ Waterproof bags for gear

_____ Tide chart

_____ Water

_____ Food (for camping or long trips)

_____ Long shirt and pants for sun and bug protection

_____ Wide-brimmed hat

_____ Shoes

_____ Wrist watch for figuring tides

_____ Sunglasses

_____ Sunscreen

_____ Insect repellent

# Safety Tips

Watch the time. Half your time up? Turn around. Plan to be back before dark.

Check the weather forecast and conditions before departing. If a storm threatens, head for shelter. If you cannot reach land, stay low in your canoe to avoid becoming a lightning target.

# Additional Reading

Two good booklets on canoeing in the Everglades are "Boat and Canoe Camping, Everglades Backcountry & Ten Thousand Islands Region" (64 pp paper) and "Guide to the Wilderness Waterway of the Everglades National Park" (64 pp paper).

Available from **Florida National Parks & Monuments Association, Inc.**, 10 Parachute Key #51, Homestead FL 33034-6735. ☎ 305-247-1216. Phone orders accepted with Visa, MasterCard, or Discover.

# Cycling Trails

Whether you want to explore for a day or a season, self-guided cycling tours are one of the best ways to discover the Everglades and the Florida Keys. Flat terrain and well marked trails lead you over miles of scenic bridges, through wildlife preserves, exotic bird sanctuaries, palm-lined beaches, and historic parks. Watersports opportunities are endless. A wide range of accommodations exist throughout the area, including picturesque oceanside campgrounds.

If historic Key West is your destination, you'll find cycling an ideal way to tour the southernmost city. Bike rentals and services are widely available. Public bike racks are everywhere.

Traffic along US Route 1, the main highway through the Keys, once posed a serious danger to road riders. Today's cyclists find wider shoulders on the bridges and a well-marked bike trail for most of the 106-mile route between Key Largo and Key West. The main road and bicycling trails through Everglades National Park are well maintained.

## Planning Your Tour

### WHEN TO GO

Visit Everglades National Park from December through March. The rest of the year brings torrential downpours and thick clouds of mosquitoes. Tour the Florida Keys between December and May. Skies are predictably sunny and air temperatures range from 75 to 85°F.

## EQUIPMENT

In South Florida, single-speed, coaster-brake bikes are as good as hi-tech 21-speed mountain bikes. Most of the land is flat, lying just a few feet above sea level. The most uphill pedaling you'll encounter is over bridges. Rental bikes are all single-speed, with baskets. Wide tires are best for the gravel and dirt trails that alternate with paved sections. For short rides in the populated areas, tools and spare equipment are usually not necessary. If you plan long-distance road riding, carry equipment sufficient to repair and inflate a tire, a spare inner-tube, some cash, sunblock, a first aid kit, bug repellent and water bottle.

## CLOTHING & GEAR

Clothing should be loose and lightweight. Cotton or Spandex cycling shorts and loose shirts are the best choice. The new mesh cycling fabrics, available at most bike shops, wick perspiration away from your body and keep you cool. Chafing and skin irritation in the groin area can be reduced by use of a sheepskin seat cover, available in most of the bike rental shops. The climate, relaxed atmosphere and fact that the bike trails and old bridges are free of automobile traffic sway many cyclists into wearing baseball caps or straw hats instead of safety helmets. If you do this, you are taking an unnecessary risk.

There are many new helmets designed for tropical wear that will keep you cool and protect your head and face. Insure a proper fit by shopping for one before your trip. To prevent serious injury in a fall or crash, avoid pushing the helmet back onto the top of your head.

For mid-winter travel, pack a windbreaker. An occasional cold front during the winter months has dropped temperatures as low as 40°F, though 75° is more usual.

## DEHYDRATION & HEAT STROKE

During summer and fall when midday temperatures soar beyond the comfort zone for riding, consider other activities. Plan cycling time for cooler morning or evening hours.

If you are not acclimated to hot weather riding, limit your tours to short distances and slow speeds. Avoid wearing long-sleeve jerseys and long tights, and drink plenty of cold liquids to avoid heat stroke or dehydration.

Insulated pouches such as ThermalBak or IceBak will keep drinks cool for several hours. For very short tours an insulated drink holder that clips on the handlebars may be purchased at most of the area bike shops.

Symptoms of heat exhaustion or heat stroke are weakness, headache, nausea and fainting. If such symptoms occur, seek immediate medical aid. If the person is conscious, give cold fluids and continuously wet down the skin with moist towels while enroute to a hospital.

### TRANSPORTING YOUR BICYCLE

Most airlines, bus companies and Amtrak will supply a special bicycle box which enables you to carry your bike as baggage. This, in theory, insures the bike arriving intact when you do. The box costs $12-$20. For transport, the handlebars, front wheel and pedals are removed. Or have your local bike shop box it for you before your trip. Be sure they use bubble pack or foam to protect it. Get a clear demonstration on how to put it back together.

Check to see if your airline has a pressurized baggage compartment. (All major US carriers have pressurized baggage compartments.) If not, you must deflate the tires. Unpressurized compartments will cause the tires to swell and possibly burst. This may result in rim damage. Be sure to make a reservation for your bicycle. During high travel times – holidays or peak season – when the baggage compartment is loaded with standard luggage you may be forced to ship your bike as freight.

# Florida Keys Cycling Trails

Florida's Keys welcome cyclists. A paved bike trail runs much of the route from Key Largo to Key West. It breaks off in some spots and crosses US 1 in places. The bridges have wide shoulders and offer unmatched views of the Atlantic Ocean and Gulf-side bays. Fragrant orange poinciana trees shade part of the bike path.

If you are starting from the mainland, take Card Sound Road from Homestead to Route 905 in Key Largo. This connects with and bypasses almost 30 miles of US 1. About 15 miles into Key Largo you pick up a paved bike trail on the ocean side of the highway. Greyhound will transport you and your boxed bike to any point along US 1 from the airport-vicinity terminal.

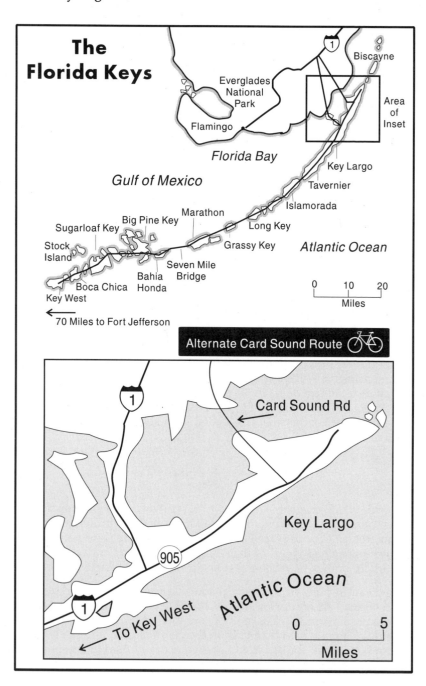

**The Florida Keys**

Biscayne

Everglades National Park

Area of Inset

Flamingo

Florida Bay

Gulf of Mexico

Key Largo

Tavernier

Islamorada

Marathon

Big Pine Key

Long Key

Sugarloaf Key

Grassy Key

Atlantic Ocean

Stock Island

Seven Mile Bridge

Bahia Honda

Boca Chica

Key West

0   10   20
Miles

← 70 Miles to Fort Jefferson

Alternate Card Sound Route

1

Card Sound Rd

Key Largo

905

Atlantic Ocean

1

To Key West ←

0   5
Miles

Finding your way around is easy; mile markers (green signs with white numbers) are posted each mile along US 1 throughout Florida's Keys. They start with 126, just south of Florida City and end with the zero marker at the corner of Fleming and Whitehead streets in Key West.

## KEY LARGO & THE UPPER KEYS

Key Largo is often the focus of a Florida Keys vacation. The bike trail begins at mile marker 106. Heading south, you'll pass a long stretch of trailers and billboards offering diving, snorkeling and fishing. All along US 1 you can rent boats, jet skis or stop to relax at waterfront resorts or restaurants. Dive shops are everywhere. At **The Italian Fisherman**, a large marina, restaurant and beach complex at MM 104, you can take a swim in the bay or the pool, rent a windsurfer, sailboat or jet ski.

A left turn at MM 103.2 brings you to the **Key Largo Undersea Park**, the sight of the first underwater hotel, **Jules' Undersea Lodge**. Currently operating as a research habitat, the hotel sits 30 feet below the surface. Non-divers must take a three-hour course before being allowed to enter the hotel using a hookah, a 120-ft-long breathing line with regulators attached. Surface compressors pump air through the lines into the hotel.

Or for a small fee you can snorkel the lagoon (use of equipment included in entrance fee), though a better choice for a snorkeling tour would be an ocean reef trip, offered each morning and afternoon at nearby **John Pennekamp Coral Reef State Park** for $32. To enter the park turn left at the sign at MM 102.5. The park offers oceanside camping, picnic areas, showers, rest rooms, bike racks, a dive shop, reef trips, snack bar, aquarium, and gift shop. It has two protected swimming beaches, sailboat, powerboat and canoe rentals, glass-bottom boat rides and a nature walk. Reservations for camping at John Pennekamp should be made in advance. For information, write to John Pennekamp Coral Reef State Park, P.O. Box 1560, Key Largo FL 33037 or ☎ 305-451-1621.

At MM 102 you'll pass **The Quay** on the bay side of the highway. The Quay offers a formal indoor/outdoor restaurant and an informal beach-side mesquite grill, a bayside pool, a small beach and a relaxing atmosphere. Sunset birdwatch cruises leave from the Quay dock.

Continuing south, the bike path leads to the Holiday Inn docks at MM 100, home of the *African Queen*, made famous by Humphrey Bogart and Katherine Hepburn in the 1951 film classic of the same name. At MM 99.5, just past the shopping center, the highway splits around a median. After passing the traffic light, keep to the left on the southbound side.

Key Largo ends at the Tavernier Creek Bridge, MM 91. The bike path stops, but you can ride on the old highway to your left. Be careful. Automobiles use this as a secondary road. On the bay side you'll find a snack bar, dive shop and boat rentals at the **Tavernier Creek Marina**. A left turn onto Burton Drive at MM 92.6 leads to **Harry Harris County Park**, a good spot for a swim and a picnic. The park opens at 8 am.

The Snake Creek Bridge, MM 87, crosses to Windley Key and Islamorada, where you can sign up for a snorkel trip to explore the sunken Spanish ship, *Herrara*, or swim with dolphins at **Theatre of the Sea** (MM 85.5). Plan a long stop at **Holiday Isle**, a beach complex at MM 84 that throbs with the beat of live reggae bands amidst the sweet smell of barbecued ribs and cotton candy. Stretch out on the white sand beach, sail, sunbathe, snorkel, fish, scuba, jet-ski, windsurf, parasail, swim or rent an inflatable island and drift off to sea. Amenities include tropical pools, rooftop and beach-side restaurants, hotels, motels and nightly entertainment.

At MM 78.5, a 24-passenger boat leaves for **Indian Key**, a historic preserve and **Lignumvitae Key**, a state botanical site. From Islamorada (also known as Upper Matecumbe Key) ride south over Teatable Bridge and Indian Key Bridge to **Lower Matecumbe Key**. **Fiesta Key** (MM 70) features a KOA Campground with tent and RV sites, a game room, laundry, two Jacuzzis, and a camp store. There are motels and resorts nearby too.

For oceanside tent camping, continue another mile and a half to **Long Key State Park** at MM 67.5. The park opens at 8 am and closes at sunset year-round. Here you can swim or fish in the Atlantic and enjoy a hike on the nature trail. Watch for fast-growing tree roots that occasionally surface through the pavement along the bike trail outside the park.

## THE MIDDLE KEYS

The Marathon area begins the Middle Keys – from Conch Key (MM 62.5) to the Seven Mile Bridge (MM 47).

Leaving Long Key Park toward Key West, you cross a 2½-mile bridge to Conch Key and Grassy Key. Salty breezes cool you and there are splendid ocean and bay views. Just beyond the bridge on Duck Key (MM 61) lies **Hawk's Cay Marina**, an oasis offering glass-bottom boat tours, boat rentals, diving, snorkeling and fishing charters. The sprawling marina/resort has 177 spacious rooms, a sandy beach, swimming lagoon and four restaurants. Bike rentals available for day trippers.

Next comes Grassy Key, MM 59, home base to the **Dolphin Research Center**, which offers unique educational programs including backcountry field trips and dolphin swims. For the next few miles the bike path winds along mangrove swamps that edge the highway. Be sure to stock up on cold beverages as there are few commercial establishments until you reach the **Days Inn & Marina** at MM 54, where you will find suntan lotion, postcards and stamps for sale. Bike rentals too.

Stop by the **Equipment Locker Sport & Cycle Shop** (MM 53) for supplies, parts or repairs. The shop rents beach cruiser bikes and kids' bikes. ☎ 305-289-1670. The bike path passes Marathon airport at MM 52 and on through the **City of Marathon**, a bustling resort community with sportfishing as the main attraction, several restaurants and motel accommodations. A left at MM 50 onto Sombrero Beach Road, followed by a two-mile ride, leads to **Sombrero Beach Park**'s picnic areas, rest rooms and ocean swimming beach. As you continue toward Key West, the sea turns a prettier shade of turquoise, the scenery gets better and the smell of salt in the air grows stronger. Seagulls and pelicans perch on the bridge railings. Sweeping ocean panoramas offer dramatic photo opportunities.

## LOWER KEYS

MM 47 begins the Seven Mile Bridge and the Lower Keys, a natural wilderness area. If you are touring locally and don't wish to cross all seven miles of bridge, travel along the adjacent old bridge. Auto

## PROTECT KEY DEER

Though they are hard to resist, pass up any desire to offer food to the pint-sized Key deer in the lower Keys. Feeding lures them onto the roadway, where many have been struck by cars.

traffic is not permitted and you'll usually find other cyclists, especially on a weekend. If you are traveling to the lower keys and Key West, the old bridge won't get you there. It stops after a few miles. Instead travel along the shoulder of the new automobile bridge. The bike trail area before the bridge is patchy with gravel and grass. It becomes a grassy shoulder after the bridge, more level on the bayside.

**Little Duck Key** (MM40), the first patch of land after crossing the Seven Mile Bridge, welcomes travelers with a lovely, small sand beach and shaded picnic tables. This is a fine spot to peel off some clothing and take a swim. Two more bridges pass over **Missouri Key** and **Sunshine Key** (formerly Ohio Key), a 75-acre camping island at MM 39. The sprawling campground features 400 sites, a marina, grocery store, tennis courts, pool, and every other imaginable amenity. Write to Sunshine Key Camping Resort, Box 790, Sunshine Key FL 33040. ☎ 305-872-2217.

At MM 38, the trail enters **Bahia Honda State Park**. Named for its "deep bay" by the Spanish, the park is one of the prettiest in the keys. It caters to 200,000 day visitors per year. Swimming sites are on the Atlantic and Gulf sides; both beaches have sandy bottoms. It also has bay- and ocean-side camp sites, a nature trail, marina and dive shop.

There are three furnished duplex cabins (six units) in the park that accommodate eight people each. Linens and utensils are provided. Snacks and limited grocery items are available at the concession building. Shaded picnic tables are at the old bridge and at Sandspur Beach. The park opens at 8 am and closes at sunset. For further information write Bahia Honda State Recreation Area, Box 782, Big Pine Key FL 33043. ☎ 305-872-2353.

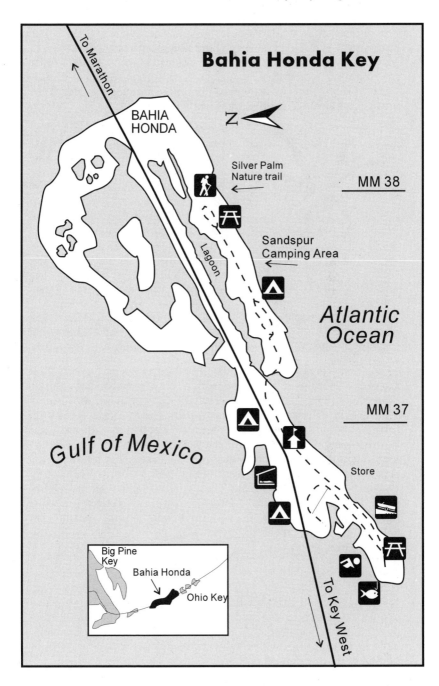

**Bahia Honda Key**

BAHIA
HONDA

To Marathon

N

Silver Palm
Nature trail

MM 38

Lagoon

Sandspur
Camping Area

Atlantic
Ocean

Gulf of Mexico

MM 37

Store

Big Pine
Key

Bahia Honda

Ohio Key

To Key West

The Bahia Honda Bridge crosses to Summerland Key (MM 35), a jumping-off point to explore offshore **Looe Key Marine Sanctuary**. MM 33 begins **Big Pine Key**, a pine forest island complete with free-roaming miniature Key deer. A right turn on Key Deer Boulevard (MM 30.5) will bring you to the refuge area for the deer. This area is also a refuge for the great white heron.

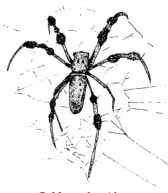

*Golden orb spider.*

After the turn-off from US 1, stay on the south side of the street, where green striping marks the bike trail. Refuge headquarters lie two miles off to the left on Watson Boulevard. If you ride another mile and a half down Key Deer Boulevard and turn left onto Big Pine Street, the path cuts into thick stands of pine and palm trees toward the Blue Hole, where several large alligators make their home. You may have trouble spotting the tiny, two-foot-high Key deer. They come out only at dusk and early morning. Watch for huge webs of golden orb spiders in the hardwood forest.

There are 25 miles of low, wet ground, mangroves and RV parks between Big Pine Key and Key West. The bike path is intermittent, with grassy or gravel shoulders. The incline in a few spots will force you to ride on the highway for a bit. Keep to the side as much as possible. You can see coral patches and distant mangrove islands from the bridges and there are spots to stop and take a swim. Avoid exploring dirt roads leading into back woods. At MM 28.5, **Parmer's Place** (☎ 305-872-2157) rents comfortable waterfront cottages. **Sugarloaf Key**, MM 20, has a resort with a dolphin show, boat ramp and comfortable air conditioned rooms. At MM 17, behind the Sugarloaf Lodge, stands a vacant bat tower, a remnant of a failed attempt to lure mosquito-hungry bats into the area.

Just past the Saddlebunch Keys, the bike path picks up on the bay side. Big Coppitt Key (MM 11-MM 7) is home base to the **Key West Naval Air Station** at Boca Chica, where thundering F-18s slice the sky above. Nearer to earth, low-flying ospreys stand quiet guard over their pole-top nests. Another mile brings you to **Stock Island**, your final approach to Key West. Named for cows and pigs kept here in early days, the island is partially a service area for municipal offices and the site of the Lower Keys hospital.

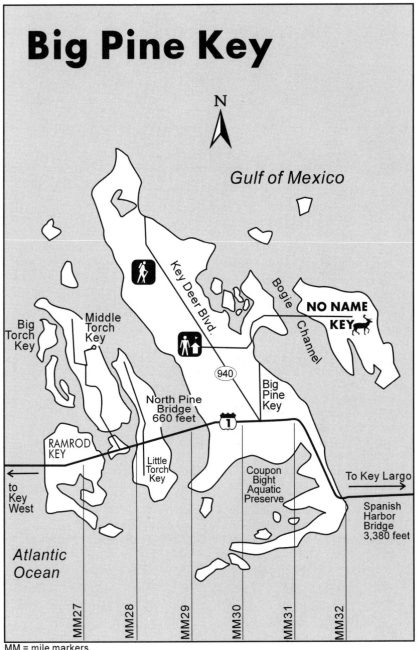

# Big Pine Key

N

Gulf of Mexico

Key Deer Blvd.

Bogie Channel

NO NAME KEY

Big Torch Key

Middle Torch Key

940

Big Pine Key

North Pine Bridge 660 feet

1

RAMROD KEY

Little Torch Key

Coupon Bight Aquatic Preserve

To Key Largo

to Key West

Spanish Harbor Bridge 3,380 feet

Atlantic Ocean

MM27

MM28

MM29

MM30

MM31

MM32

MM = mile markers

*The longest segmented bridge in the world, the famous Seven Mile Bridge is one of 43 bridges that comprise the 113-mile Overseas Highway in the Florida Keys.*

A right turn onto Junior College Road, just before the Key West Bridge, will bring you to the Key West Seaplane Base where you can charter a half-day snorkeling excursion to Fort Jefferson. The Key West Resort Golf Course, Tennessee Williams Fine Arts Center, and Florida Keys Hospital share the island.

### KEY WEST

After crossing the bridge into Key West you can turn left or right onto a paved bike trail that skirts the shoreline on both North and South Roosevelt Boulevards. Either route will lead you to the historic heart of Florida's Keys, Old Town Key West. If you arrive by car, boat, ship or plane you'll find rental bikes at hotels and in town. Cycle touring is the favored way to avoid congested traffic and tour the city. Open cabs are cyclist-powered.

A right turn off the Key West Bridge brings you past a commercial strip of hotels and restaurants, Garrison's Bight and the Key West Yacht Club. Farther on, North Roosevelt turns into Truman Avenue. Truman later intersects Duval Street, which leads to the historic section. The bike path ends with North Roosevelt Boulevard, but picks up again on the south side of the island at Higgs Beach.

A right turn on Whitehead Street leads to Mallory Square and the center of activity. Be sure to obey the one-way street signs as cyclists are ticketed for going the wrong way. A left turn at the Key West Bridge along South Roosevelt Boulevard brings you past the airport, the Salt Pond – an ecological preserve and new condo development, Smathers Beach and Higgs Beach. The bike path stops at the south end of Higgs Beach. A right turn will lead to

Truman Avenue. The area on and around Caroline Street is shaded by huge tropical poinciana and palm trees. Stop by the Chamber of Commerce on Wall Street in the Mallory Square area for a copy of the *Solares Hill Walking and Biking Guide* that details every inch of the city. Additional bike paths throughout the city are in the planning stages.

## Key West Bicycle Rentals

*(Most accept major credit cards)*

**Adventure Scooter & Bicycle Rentals** features daily specials, locks, group rates, with locations all over town:

2900 N. Roosevelt Blvd, in the Blockbuster Video & K-Mart Shopping Center at Key Plaza. ☎ 293-9933.

505 Greene St., across from Sloppy Joe's. ☎ 296-5552.

3675 S. Roosevelt Blvd. at the Key Wester Resort next to Airport. ☎ 293-9922.

3824 N. Roosevelt Blvd., at the Comfort Inn next to Key West Welcome Center. ☎ 292-1666.

601 Front St., Hyatt Key West. ☎ 293-9944.

617 Front St., at the Galleon Resort. ☎ 293-9955.

1 Duval St., Pier House. ☎ 293-0441.

925 Duval St., corner of Truman and Duval. ☎ 293-9911.

201 Front St., Pier B, in Truman Annex at cruise ship docks. ☎ 296-0391.

**Bike Key West** provides a backpack, lock and helmet with each rental. Open Mon. through Fri., 9 am to 6 pm. Free pick-up and delivery. ☎ 305-292-9165.

**Bicycle Therapy Extreme** extends free pickup and delivery from two locations:

1019 White St, by Fausto's. ☎ 293-8479.

1011 Truman Ave, near Grinnel and Truman. ☎ 294-0243.

**The Bicycle Center** offers three-speed cruisers, mopeds and scooters. 523 Truman Ave. ☎ 294-4556.

**Bubba's Bike Rental**, 705 Duval St. ☎ 294-2618.

**The Bike Shop** specializes in expert repairs on all makes and models with the largest selection of parts and accessories in the Keys; free estimates. Open Mon.-Sat., 9 am-5:30 pm.; Sun., 10 am-5:30 pm. 1110 Truman Ave. ☎ 294-1073.

**Caribbean Scooter Rental,** 3031 N. Roosevelt Blvd. ☎ 293-9971.

**Conch Bike Express** delivers to your hotel, condo, marina or home. All bikes have a basket and lock. ☎ 294-4318.

**Moped Hospital** offers group rates on bicycle and moped rentals, with "easy to ride" lady's models. 601 Truman Ave. ☎ 296-3344.

**Key West Bike Co,** 2401 N. Roosevelt Blvd. ☎ 292-0046.

**Keys Moped & Scooter Inc.,** 523 Truman Ave. ☎ 294-0399.

**Laskooters,** 1313 Simonton St. ☎ 296-7692.

**Paradise Rentals, Inc.** at La Concha Holiday Inn, 430 Duval St. ☎ 292-6441. Or at Key West Sandal Factory, 105 Whitehead St. ☎ 296-0909.

**Pirate Scooter,** open seven days from 8 am to 8 pm, offers helmets and locks, free instruction and free pickup and delivery anywhere in Key West. Three locations:

817 Simonton St., Old Town. ☎ 295-0000.

3820 N. Roosevelt Blvd., EconoLodge. ☎ 295-0000.

3852 N. Roosevelt Blvd., Day's Inn. ☎ 295-0000.

**Scooter Safari,** 3706 N. Roosevelt Blvd. ☎ 294-4420.

**Sun-N-Fun,** 1316 Duval St. ☎ 296-1543.

**Tropical Bicycle & Scooter Rentals** offers beach cruisers, scooters and jeeps. Open seven days. 1300 Duval St. ☎ 294-8136.

# Cycling Everglades National Park

The main park entrance is 45 miles from Miami International Airport. There are no regularly scheduled bus tours or public transportation to or within the park, but Greyhound Bus Company will take you along Route 1 to Route 9336, Florida City, which is 11 miles from the main park entrance. From there you can cycle route 9336 – a paved road through a residential and farm area. Signs on the highway will point you in the proper direction – a right turnoff from the southbound lane onto 9336. Greyhound buses leave three times daily from the airport vicinity bus station located at 4111 N.W. 27 Street, Miami FL 33142, ☎ 305-876-7123, and the Homestead terminal at 5 N.E. 3rd Road, Homestead FL 33030, ☎ 305-247-2040.

Avoid cycling the entire distance from the airport. There is no shoulder, and traffic is fast-moving and heavy. Transporting your bike by bus or car is a safer choice.

There is an entrance fee that is good for seven days: $5 per private motorized vehicle or $2 per person entering by bicycle. At the Main Visitor Center, open daily from 8 am till 5 pm, you can view a 15-minute introductory film and displays, plus you can pick up schedules of park activities. Books, postcards, insect repellent and other items are sold here.

The main park road begins at the Visitor Center, wanders through the Pinelands and ends 38 miles later at Flamingo. The road is paved and well-maintained although no services are available. Several cycling trails take off from this road and a few more begin at Flamingo. Horseback riders occasionally use these trails. Use caution and quietly give them the right-of-way when passing. The north end of the park can be best explored along Shark Valley Loop.

If transporting your bike to the Everglades by car, you may park at the Royal Palm Visitor Center parking lot, Long Pine Key picnic area or Flamingo Outpost. If you plan to camp, you will need a backcountry permit, available free at the Main Visitor Center. The only overnight visitor accommodations within the park are at Flamingo Lodge, located 38 miles southwest of the Main Visitor Center.

Camping is on a first-come, first-served basis. Flamingo has 60 tent sites and 235 drive-in sites. Long Pine Key has 108 sites. During the winter, campgrounds fill every night. Plan to arrive early in the day.

Modern comfort stations and drinking water are available at both sites; cold-water showers only at Flamingo. Limited groceries and camping supplies may be purchased at the Flamingo Marina Store. Swimming in the park is discouraged. Fresh water ponds have alligators; salt water areas are shallow with mucky bottoms. Underwater visibility is extremely poor and sharks and barracudas abound.

# Everglades National Park Cycling Trails

**Shark Valley Loop**, a 15-mile road that circuits the northern portion of Everglades National Park, lies off US 41, the Tamiami Trail, 50 miles from the Main Visitor Center. This road edges a wide shallow waterway crowded with dense fields of sawgrass – the headwaters for Shark River.

Alligators, otters, deer, raccoons, frogs, snakes, turtles and birds, including rare wood storks and snail kites inhabit this watery expanse. Hardwood hammocks and other tree islands dot the landscape. The loop road, originally constructed by oil prospectors, is used for tram rides, bicycles and walking. A 65-ft observation tower along the road provides a spectacular bird's eye view.

For your safety use extreme caution when stopping for trams. The shoulder is very steep. Be sure to come to a complete stop before dismounting and pulling to the side of the road. Watch out for snakes and alligators. Venomous pygmy rattlesnakes are common on high ground during the wet season. Also avoid touching poison ivy, poisonwood trees or the sawgrass, which can inflict nasty cuts.

Bicycles may be rented next to the ticket booth daily from 8:30 am to 3 pm. Cycling along the Tamiami Trail is not recommended – traffic is fast moving, services are few and the road shoulder is soft. The Shark Valley Visitor Center opens between 8:30 am and 5:15 pm. Cycling permits are required for groups of 10 or more.

## THE PINELANDS

A network of interconnecting trails runs through the Pinelands, an unusually diverse pine forest. Under the pine canopy are about 200 types of plants, including 30 found nowhere else on Earth. Whitetail deer, opossums, raccoons and the endangered Florida panther live in the Pinelands. You can also see turtles, lizards and snakes, exotic zebra butterflies, striped grasshoppers, red-bellied woodpeckers, orchids and tree snails. The bicycle trails, a series of one-lane fire roads, are well maintained. Avoid those marked for hiking only; they may be mucky and impassable by bike.

**Mahogany Trail,** located 20 miles from the Main Visitor Center and two miles from the main  park road, is one of the favorite walking trails and worth a side trip to see. The raised boardwalk climbs first over swamp, then into a dense jungle-like environment. In contrast to the surrounding grass prairies, here you can view red-headed woodpeckers, orchids growing in the tree tops, rare paurotis palms and towering mahogany trees, including the largest living specimen in the United States. Huge golden orb spider webs are suspended from the tree branches; colorful liguus tree snails inhabit the bark. At night, barred owls awaken to hunt. No facilities.

## FLAMINGO AREA TRAILS

Flamingo sits at the south end of the park, on Florida Bay. The principal jump-off point for canoeing, fishing and boating in Everglades National Park, it is also a leader in mosquito production. Bug repellent is needed year round. In late November we were fogged in by mosquitos at the campground, but found the trails north of Flamingo and the paved area at the marina less infested.

The camp store (open mid-Nov. through mid-March) rents canoes, stocks groceries, camping supplies, bait and fuel. **Flamingo Marina and Outpost Resort** offers air-conditioned rooms, spacious cabins, camping, a pool, and gift shop, plus wilderness tours, fishing trips and tram tours. In season, you can rent a bicycle at the shack outside the camp store. ☎ 800-600-3813.

**Snake Bight Trail,** a rugged 1.6-mile route, tunnels one-way through a shaded tropical hardwood hammock. The trail starts six miles east of Flamingo from the main park road. Good bird watching exists in the wooded areas from the short boardwalk at the end of the trail. Alligators frequent this spot.

**Rowdy Bend,** a 2.6-mile trail, winds along an old roadbed through buttonwood forest and open coastal prairie. The trail is often overgrown with grasses.

# Fishing

A day of fishing anywhere is great, but in the Everglades and Florida Keys, it's better! Where else can you catch bonefish from a dock, a tarpon or permit from a bridge, a marlin from a charter boat and even sea trout in a backyard canal? Here's a rundown on what to expect offshore, back country (mangrove flats – Florida Bay and Ten Thousand Island region), from a party boat, a head boat, a bridge, and even onshore.

## Offshore

You book charter boats for a deep-sea fishing trip and they take care of the rest. Bait, tackle and ice are usually provided, along with fish – all kinds of fish from tail dancing sailfish and marlin, blackfin tuna, king mackerel or reel-smoking wahoo and colorful, fabulous dolphin (the fish, not Flipper) to delicious yellowtail and mutton snapper, grouper and kingfish, all in their season.

Florida Keys captains are professional and really aim to please. They will stay out as long as you don't give up. Key West Captain Bill Wickers' favorite tale is of a 700-lb marlin hooked from his boat, the *Linda D*, at 1:10 pm on 50-lb line. The fish put up a fight for the entire day and was brought to the boat 10 or 12 times. The angler held steady long after sunset, certain the fish would tire. At 10:30 pm the marlin let go and swam away.

*Reproduced in part with permission from an article by Bob T. Epstein.*

Charter boats cater to parties of four to six persons with full-day rates averaging about $500, half-day about $300, for everything except lunch, beverages and suntan lotion. Light tackle boats can accommodate one or two fishermen at substantially lower rates. Half-day party-boat tariffs average $25, including tackle.

In Key West where the ocean meets the Gulf there is always a calm area to fish. On the Gulf side the boats troll for barracuda, kingfish and bonito. Oceanside catches are usually sailfish and dolphin.

# Where To Book A Charter

Charter boats are widely available and may be booked through many resorts and the following marinas and guides:

### NORTH KEY LARGO

Gilbert's Motel & Marina, MM 108. ☎ 305-451-1133

Key Largo Holiday Inn Resort & Marina, MM 100 Oceanside. ☎ 305-451-3661

Tavernier Creek Marina, MM 90.5. ☎ 305-852-5854

### ISLAMORADA

Islamorada Yacht Basin/Lorelei, MM 82. ☎ 305-664-4338

Holiday Isle Resorts & Marina, MM 84. ☎ 305-664-2321

Bud N' Mary's Marina, MM 79.5. ☎ 305-664-2461

Whale Harbor Dock, MM 83.5. ☎ 305-664-4511

### MARATHON

Holiday Inn Marina, MM 54. ☎ 305-451-2121

7-Mile Marina, MM 47.5 (at Seven Mile Bridge). ☎ 305-743-7712

Faro Blanco Marine Resort, 1996 OS Hwy. ☎ 305-743-9018

Hawk's Cay Resort and Marina, MM 61, Duck Key. ☎ 305-743-9000

Key Colony Beach Marina, 589 6th St., Key Colony Beach. ☎ 305-289-1310

### KEY WEST

Land's End Marina, 201 William St., Key West . ☎ 305-296-3838

*Kayaking, Key Largo.*

*Manatee, © Sea World, Orlando.*

*Everglades pelican.*

*Great white heron, Key Largo.*

*Seaplanes at Fort Jefferson.*

*Quay Beach Club, Key Largo.*

*Duval St., Key West, at night, from La Concha rooftop.*

*Swimming with dolphins, Theatre of the Sea, Islamorada.*

*Soft corals, Key Largo.*

*Airboat, Miccosukee Indian Village.*

*Boardwalk, Corkscrew Swamp Sanctuary, Naples.*

# FISHING CALENDAR

## JANUARY-FEBRUARY

OFFSHORE (sailfish, amberjack, kingfish). REEF (snapper, grouper, mackerel, barracuda). BAY (snapper, mackerel, cobia good on wrecks). FLATS (bonefish, barracuda).

## MARCH-APRIL

OFFSHORE (sailfish, tuna, fair dolphin fish, peak season for mako shark). REEF (snapper, cobia, grouper, barracuda). BAY (good snapper, good cobia on wrecks). FLATS (bonefish, good permit, tarpon at bridges and back country flats).

## MAY-JUNE

OFFSHORE (dolphin fish, tuna, sailfish). REEF (snapper, barracuda). BAY (snapper). FLATS (bonefish, permit, excellent tarpon on flats, tarpon at bridges).

## JULY-AUGUST

OFFSHORE (dolphin fish). REEF (barracuda, excellent snapper especially at night). BAY (fair snapper, permit on Gulf wrecks). FLATS (bonefish, permit).

## SEPTEMBER-OCTOBER

OFFSHORE (dolphin fish, fair to good tuna). REEF (fair to good snapper, excellent barracuda). FLATS (good bonefish and redfish in October, fair to good tarpon and snook at bridges).

## NOVEMBER-DECEMBER

OFFSHORE (sailfish, kingfish). REEF (snapper, good mackerel, barracuda). BAY (snapper, good cobia especially on wrecks). FLATS (bonefish, good redfish, fair to good tarpon and snook at bridges).

*Cycling in Key West.*

Charter Row Amberjack, Pier North Roosevelt Ave., Garrison Bight, Key West. ☎ 305-294-3093

Oceanside Marina, 5950 Peninsual Ave., Stock Island. ☎ 305-294-4676

*For a list of Key West charterboat captains write to*: Craig Jiovani, President, Key West Charterboat Association, 2 Jay Lane, Key West FL 33040.

### EVERGLADES, TEN THOUSAND ISLAND AREA

*(All mangrove fishing from shallow-draft flats boats)*

Chokoloskee Island Park, P.O. Box 430, Chokoloskee FL 33925. ☎ 941-695-2414

Captain Tony Brock, Chokoloskee FL 33925. ☎ 941-695-4150

Captain Max Miller, Everglades City FL 33929. ☎ 941-695-2420

Captain Charles, Taverner FL. ☎ 941-695-4108

Captain Jon Shields. ☎ 941-643-6689

Captain Sophia Stiffler, Barron River Dock 164-167, Everglades City FL ☎ 941-695-1000

# Party Boats Or Head Boats

If you're interested in rubbing elbows with lots of other fishermen and want to share a fine fishing and people-watching experience, try a party boat or head boat. It's an inexpensive way to fish offshore. Bait and tackle are provided. You may even make new friends and catch dinner. Snappers, groupers, even dolphin and sailfish are caught off party boats. Sharks, too! Even in your own boat or a rental boat, offshore is a must, a real Keys experience.

### DEEP SEA PARTY BOATS
#### Key Largo

Sailor's Choice. Three trips daily, Holiday Inn Docks, MM 100. ☎ 305-451-1802, 451-0041

#### Islamorada

Robbies Holiday Isle Docks (South End), MM 84.5, Islamorada FL 33036. ☎ (docks) 305-664-8070, (office) 305-664-4196

 **CATCH & RELEASE TACTICS**

**DON'T WASTE TIME.** Quickly play and release the fish. A fish played too long may be too exhausted to recover.

**HANDLE FISH GENTLY.** Don't grip fish by the eyes or gills; use a firm grasp but don't squeeze too tightly. Never squeeze a fish around its middle.

**UNHOOK CAREFULLY.** Never rip the hook out. Grab bend of hook and turn fly upside down so the point of hook is pointing down toward the water. Squeeze down barbs on hook with pliers. When deeply hooked, a fish's chance of survival is much better if the leader is cut and the hook is left in place.

**REVIVE EXHAUSTED FISH.** Revive the fish by holding it upright in the water (heading upstream in streams) and moving it back and forth to force water through its gills. When the fish revives and begins to swim normally, let it go to survive and challenge another angler.

*Reproduced with permission from* Orvis News.

Gulf Lady Party Fishing Boat, Bud N' Mary's Marina, MM 79.5, Islamorada FL 33036. ☎ 305-664-2628/664-2461

Ms. Tradewinds, MM 83.5, Whale Harbor Marina. ☎ 305-664-8341

Captain's Lady Party Boat, MM 84.5 at Holiday Isle. ☎ 305-664-8498

Captain Winner II Party Boat, Holiday Isle. ☎ 305-664-8070

Caloosa Party Boat, Whale Harbor Marina, Holiday Isle. ☎ 664-852-3200

**Marathon**

Starlight Fishing Boat, MM 53, Winner Marina East. ☎ 305-743-6941

Winner Party Boats, MM 50, Winner Sombrero Docks. ☎ 305-664-8070

*Technique for reviving a tarpon from a boat. Hold fish upright and move forward and backward to force water through mouth and gills.*

*Technique for reviving a tarpon in the water is the same. Gently move the fish back and forth to move water through mouth and gills.*

### Key West

Capt. John's Greyhound V, City Marina/Amberjack Pier, Palm Ave & N. Roosevelt. ☎ 305-296-5139

Gulfstream III, City Marina/Amberjack Pier #8. ☎ 305-296-8494

Can't Miss Party Fishing Boat, City Marina, Pier No 2. ☎ 305-296-3751

# Back Country Fishing

### Florida Bay, Ten Thousand Islands Region

Back country is exactly what it says, out back in the wild beautiful Florida Bay, Everglades National Park, Great White Heron National Wildlife Refuge or around the uninhabited keys in the Gulf of Mexico and Ten Thousand Island region.

White Pelicans, egrets, or cormorants make a beautiful backdrop for fishing these flat waters. Folks who don't like offshore usually love the back country. Sea trout, redfish, jacks, tarpon, and snook are just some of the fish you can catch out there in "God's Country," where man's footprints are rare and nature's hand is heavy! In Everglades City, along Route 29 or the Tamiami Trail, you can fish the roadside canals wherever you find a parking space.

# Bridge & Shore Fishing

For the casual visitor who has no intention of boating due to time restrictions, is afraid of sea sickness, who has small children or is sunburn-prone, fishing from shore or a bridge is for you. Snapper, grouper, sheepshead, permit and even tarpon can be and are caught from the Keys bridges. There are more than two dozen bridges that accommodate fishermen and sightseers. You can watch pelicans, egrets, seagulls and osprey feed and preen their feathers only feet away. Here, too, the people are friendly and the sights are varied. It can be really exciting, especially when a fisherman hooks up with the "silver king," and the tarpon zooms parallel to the bridge. Everyone moves very quickly, as a hundred pounds or more of shimmering beauty and strength tests the angler. All who witness get to see a battle with a sporting giant of the fish clan, the tarpon. Fishing from shore, or wading with lures or bait, you can catch the spectacular bonefish or hook a barracuda. For the neophyte, a toothy and tough 'cuda is fun, but not difficult to entice. Whatever your fishing pleasure, you won't be disappointed in the Everglades or Florida Keys.

A much-applauded new trend that many Floridian fishermen are practicing is a catch-and-release policy for "trophy fish" that were previously killed for wall mounting.

"It insures some good fishing for our grandchildren," remarked one charter captain. Many Keys marinas feature lifelike replicas of favorite gamefish so anglers need no kill to go home with a photo of their catch. The International Gamefish Release and Enhancement Foundation, Inc. is a non-profit organization with the goal of encouraging releases. Their credo: "It takes a good fisherman to catch a fish, but it takes a great fisherman to release it."

# Fly Fishing Schools

**Orvis Fly Fishing School** holds three-day weekend classes in northern Key Largo throughout March and April of each year. Experienced fly-fishing instructors share their secrets of stalking and catching the world's most prized game fish. The current fee of $395 includes comprehensive instruction, a non-resident fishing license if required, lunches, use of an Orvis rod, reel, line, leaders and flies, plus your choice of an Orvis fly fishing guide book. Accommodation packages available. Call for information and reservations, ☎ 800-235-9763.

 **HELP UNHOOK A PELICAN**

Wherever you fish, a hungry pelican will show up looking for a handout. But they do not know how to avoid fishhooks or lines and often get ensnared. If you just cut the line, you are condemning the bird to entanglement and starvation. Do not be afraid if you get a pelican on your line.

REEL IN THE BIRD. GRAB ITS BILL. FOLD UP THE WINGS. THEN BRING IT TO, OR CALL, THE NEAREST WILDLIFE RESCUE CENTER.

## PELICAN RESCUE STEPS

### 1. REEL IN PELICAN HOOKED ON YOUR LINE.

Reel in your line smoothly and firmly. Be careful not to break the line. Even though the bird is struggling and flapping its wings, it only weighs about six pounds and is really quite harmless when handled properly.

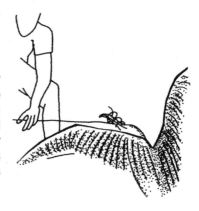

### 2. GRAB THE BILL.

When the bird is close to you, grab part or all of the bill. Close it and hold it securely in one hand. The inside edges of the bill are sharp but, unless you rub your hand up and down the edge, a pelican bite will not hurt you.

**3. FOLD UP THE WINGS**. Fold the wings into their normal closed position and hold them there. This quiets down the bird and it should stop struggling.

**4. HOLD THE BIRD AND TRANSPORT IT TO THE NEAREST CENTER.**

Turn the bird's head around so it lies along the middle of its back (that's how pelicans sleep) and so it's easier to handle. Transport it on your lap to the nearest wildlife rescue center. KEEP A FIRM GRIP ON THE BIRD'S BILL.

**5. TAKE THE BIRD TO ONE OF THE FOLLOWING RESCUE CENTERS:**

UPPER KEYS. Florida Keys Wild Bird Center, MM 93.6, Key Largo. ☎ 305-852-4486.

MIDDLE KEYS. Knight's Key Campground, MM 47, Marathon. ☎ 305-743-7373.

LOWER KEYS. Wildlife Rescue of the Florida Keys Indigenous Park, Whitehead St., Key West. ☎ 305-294-1414.

Note: The wild bird rescue centers receive no government funding and depend solely on donations. If you wish to make a tax-deductible contribution, checks should be made out to FKWBC.

*Reproduced with permission from material provided by the Florida Keys Wild Bird Center. Drawings adapted with permission from illustrations by Kelly Grinter.*

*Hammerhead shark.*

**The Florida Keys Fly Fishing School** provides fly fishermen of all skill levels with an opportunity to learn or improve their saltwater fly fishing skills and techniques. The school specializes in catching the tropical flats species such as tarpon, bonefish, snook, permit, redfish and mutton snapper by sight fishing with fly rods on the flats. The classes are usually held at Cheeca Lodge (☎ 800-327-2888) in Islamorada. They do not include actual fishing, but cover casting, sighting fish, fly selection, fly tying, fly presentation, tackle specification and selection, leaders, knots, fighting fish, wind problems, flats etiquette, short and quick casting, selecting fly fishing guides and more. Films, slides, and field exercises are used to give broad coverage. Students are given plenty of personal attention.

The instructor staff is a "Who's Who" of saltwater fly fishermen, including Stu Apte, author of *Fishing in the Florida Keys and Flamingo*, Chico Fernandez, Steve Huff, Rick Ruoff, Steve Rajeff, Flip Pallot and Sandy Moret. All of the instructor staff are known for their tremendous angling ability and a unique desire to share with someone who seeks an ultimate angling experience. The weekend sessions provide at least one instructor for every five students. The seminars are held six weekends per year at Cheeca Lodge beginning with a Friday evening reception and ending on Sunday afternoon. The $750 fee includes the course, breakfast and lunch for two days, and use of equipment. Advanced courses are in the planning stage.

For yearly schedules write to Sandy Moret, Director, Florida Keys Fly Fishing School, P.O. Box 603, Islamorada FL 33036. ☎ 305-664-5423.

# Fishing Guides

Lists and specialty fishing guides may be contacted through the following associations. Rates start at $200 per day.

**Florida Keys Fishing Guides Association**, P.O. Box 936, Islamorada FL 33036

**Marathon Fishing Guides Association**, P.O. Box 500065, Marathon FL 33050

**Islamorada Fishing Guides Association**, Mike Collins, President, P.O. Box 803, Islamorada FL 33036

**Key West Charterboat Association**, Craig Jiovani, President, 2 Jay Lane, Key West FL 33040

# Fishing on Your Own

For visiting anglers who trailer their own small fishing craft, there are public ramps everywhere. Numerous tackle and bait shops are throughout the area for do-it-yourself anglers. Small boaters fishing the reefs and wrecks will find abundant marine life on the shallow patch reefs on the Gulf side of the Keys and Everglades. On the ocean side there is excellent fishing over the coral reefs and shipwrecks, with yellowtail, mangrove and mutton snapper, grouper and cobia. Mutton snapper up to 12 lbs have been caught by Key West reef fishermen. In the small bays around Flamingo, the southern tip of Everglades National Park, especially Snake Bight, you have a chance for redfish, snapper or sea trout.

All boat operators should be familiar with the nautical traffic laws. These rules prevent collisions at sea. They can be obtained from any US Coast Guard Auxiliary.

Boats under power should never approach closer than 100 yards of another boat or float displaying a diver-down flag except at idle speed and using great caution. Not all nautical hazards are marked by bouys and markers. Consult charts at dive shops, marinas and marine stores. Boaters utilizing Lo-

*Mangrove fishing.*

# HOW TO HANDLE OTHER BIRDS

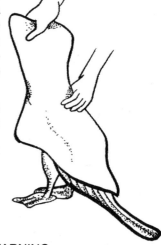

Toss a towel or shirt over the bird's head and firmly grasp its bill in a closed position. Gently fold the wings into their normal position and transport the bird to the nearest wildlife rescue center (see page 95).

Covering any bird's head will help to keep the bird calm, reducing its struggling efforts.

*Great blue heron.*

WARNING:

BEFORE attempting to catch a heron, PUT ON A PAIR OF PROTECTIVE GLASSES. Herons defend themselves by lunging for the eyes.

ran-C for navigation should recalibrate their equipment for this particular area.

A series of mooring buoys have been placed in high-use areas within the marine parks. The buoy system was developed to reduce anchor damage to the coral and provide a convenient means of securing your boat. The buoys are available on a first-come, first-served basis for everyone.

When approaching the buoys, watch for snorkelers, divers and swimmers. Approach from downwind or down-current and secure your boat to a pick-up line attached to the other end of the buoy.

# Fishing Regulations

As of January 1, 1990 a recreational saltwater fishing license has been required for Florida residents and nonresidents. The license is required for taking, attempting to take or possessing marine fish. These include finfish species as well as marine invertebrates. Examples of finfish are hogfish, sharks, trout, mackerel, rays, catfish, eels and tarpon. Marine invertebrates include snails, whelks, clams, scallops, shrimp, crab, lobster, sea stars, sea urchins and sea cucumbers. Unless you are a Florida resident fishing from shore or from a pier which has a valid pier saltwater fishing license or is fixed to the land, saltwater fishing licenses are required of all age 16 and older. Also included are all Florida residents 16 to 65 years of age who fish from a boat, float, or place they have reached by boat, float, swimming or snorkeling. If you are on a charter boat or with a licensed fishing guide you are covered by the guide's license. Crawfish and snook stamps are required for possession of either. Lobsters (crawfish) are protected year-round in some areas of Dade and Monroe counties. Sportsman's mini-season is the last full weekend prior to August 1 (two days only).

Saltwater fishing licenses are sold at all county tax collectors' offices and at many bait and tackle shops. Rates at this writing are: three-day non-resident, $5, 7-day $15. Residents pay $10 for 10 days, $12 for one year, $60 for five years.

For updated licensing information contact the **Marine Patrol District** office: District 2 – Miami, Port Everglades, ☎ 305-325-3346; District 3 – Marathon, ☎ 305-289-2323.

Freshwater fishing licenses are required to fish the freshwater fish in the canals along the Tamiami Trail and the Everglades. Licenses and regulations are available from the marina shops and most bait and tackle shops.

*Wood storks,*
*Corkscrew Sanctuary.*

# Nature Hikes & Walks

State and national parks throughout the Florida Keys and Everglades provide informative walking programs including "slogs" or wet hikes though water and mud where you "taste and smell the rich odors of the swamp," beach walks to observe sea grasses, tidal pools, sponges and wading-bird habitats, woodland hikes, bird-watching and out-island tours to examine fossilized coral or virgin tropical forests.

Many parks have raised boardwalks that climb over tidal flats, sawgrass prairies and fragrant mangrove swamps. Patient observers discover spectacular sights and sounds – croaking frogs and alligators, pods of dolphins splashing across the horizon to soaring bald eagles, colonies of nesting wood storks or flocks of egrets gorging on fish.

Florida Keys trails are accessible throughout the year, but the best time for exploring the Everglades is Florida's dry season, mid-December through mid-April. The rest of the year brings a chance of torrential downpours that wash out many of the low-lying trails. Precipitation can exceed 50 inches a year. After a rainfall mosquitoes, sandflies and other biting insects thicken the air.

Wildlife in the Everglades becomes more difficult to spot in summer. During winter's dry season, birds and other wildlife congregate in and around the waterholes, conveniently visible from the nature trails. These life-rich holes, cleared out of the Everglades' limestone bed by the alligators, are a breeding ground for small fish, turtles and snails, which, in turn, become food for alligators, birds and mammals until the rains come.

Hammocks, mentioned throughout this chapter, are isolated stands of hardwoods and plants that contrast with the surrounding plant life. These botanical showplaces, often islands of tropical hardwoods shading orchids and ferns in the middle of a sawgrass prairie, are vulnerable to floods, fires and invasions of saline waters. Hammocks form on a ridge or elevated mound of earth.

## Florida Keys Nature Hikes

*denotes handicap access

**John Pennekamp State Park\***, located at MM 102.5, features two nature trails. One starts at the parking lot across from the Visitor's Center and leads through a tropical hammock, home to raccoons and woodland birds. The other, an elevated mangrove trail that begins in the parking lot across from the Picnic Pavilion, offers a close encounter with an array of wading birds – herons, egrets, ducks, cormorants and coots. The park offers interpretive programs, canoe and kayak rentals, boat rentals, and ocean tours.

**Lignumvitae Key**, a 280-acre island on the Gulf side of Islamorada, is a virgin tropical forest accessible by charter boat. Isolated in time and space relative to the other keys, Lignumvitae Key was first settled by financier William Matheson, who built a four-bedroom coral-rock house on it in 1919, but left the rest of the island alone, except for a small clearing and boat dock. The State of Florida acquired the key in 1972 and made it a protected state botanical site. Today the house serves as a visitor's center. State park rangers conduct guided tours three times daily, Thursday-Monday.

On the tour, rangers identify lignum vitae, mahogany, strangler fig, poisonwood, pigeon plum and gumbo limbo trees. Fifty people may explore the key at one time, 25 on the nature trail and 25 in the clearing. Walking shoes and mosquito repellent are recommended. Book a trip at the MM 78.5 boat ramp. ☎ 305-664-4815.

**Indian Key State Historical Site**, a 12-acre island on the ocean side of Islamorada, features ruins of a wreckers' village burned down by Indians in 1840 and numerous sisal plants cultivated by famed botanist, Dr. Henry Perrine. Book a guided walking tour with the Florida Park Service at the MM 78.5 boat ramp. ☎ 305-664-4815.

**Long Key State Park\*** at MM 67.5 supports an abundant wading-bird population. The main trail originates on the ocean side near the observation tower, then winds through beach areas and across a mangrove-lined lagoon. Signs along the boardwalk interpret the lagoon. Park rangers present campfire programs and lead guided walks year-round. The park opens at 8 am and closes at sunset.

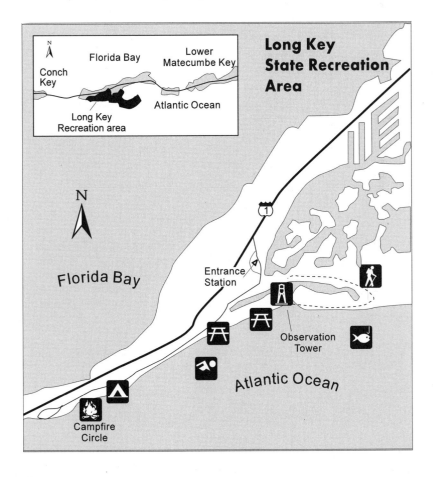

*Key deer.*

**Crane Point Hammock**, located at MM 50, contains the last virgin palm hammock in North America. Noted as an environmental and archaeological site, the 63-acre tract once sheltered an entire Bahamian village. An 1800's "Indian-and-hurricane-proof" home built with two-foot-thick walls stands on the grounds. Pre-Columbian and prehistoric Indian artifacts have been found here.

Enter the sanctuary through the **Museum of Natural History of the Florida Keys**, 5550 Overseas Highway, Marathon. It features 20 major exhibits and six rotating displays covering the geography, botany and zoology of the Keys. The trail runs a quarter-mile through a pit exposing ancient coral fossils, rare hardwoods, native palms and red mangroves. Crane Point Hammock and its museum are open 9 am to 5 pm, Wednesday through Monday. ☎ 305-743-9100.

**Bahia Honda State Park**, at MM 36.5, displays rare plants not often found on the other islands including the satinwood tree, spiny catesbaea and dwarf morning glory. A nature trail at the far end of the park's Sandspur Beach, oceanside, follows the shore of a tidal lagoon, then twists through a coastal strand hammock and back along the beach. Bird life includes the white-crowned pigeon, great white heron, roseate spoonbill, reddish egret, osprey, brown pelican and least tern.

Guided walks are available to groups by reservation. ☎ 305-872-2353. Park tours and boat rentals, ☎ 305-872-1127.

The **Big Pine Key Walking Trail** starts 1½ miles north of the intersection of Key Deer Boulevard and Watson Boulevard. It winds for two-thirds of a mile through slash pine and palms adjoining Watson Hammock, a unique hardwood area which is also habitat for a variety of tree cactus and a species of prickly pear not seen anywhere else in the world. The trail lies within the **Key Deer Refuge**, home of tiny deer measuring 24-32 inches at the shoulder and weighing 45-75 pounds. Fawns weigh two to four pounds with a hoof the size of a thumbnail. Rangers ask that you don't feed the deer. A few alligators reside in the Blue Hole, a nearby old rock quarry.

## Everglades Hiking Trails

Many hiking trails in Everglades National Park branch from the Main Park Road, which begins at the Main Visitor Center and ends 38 miles later at Flamingo. These paths range from easy walks of less than a quarter-mile to more strenuous ones up to 14 miles long. If hiking off the trails, let someone know your schedule and planned route before you leave. Footpaths marked by an asterisk indicate access for the handicapped.

Watch for poisonous snakes, including coral snakes, water moccasins, diamondback and pygmy rattlers. Do not damage, remove, or disturb any plants. Like the animals, they are protected and some are poisonous – poison ivy, poison wood and manchineel. Pets are not allowed on the trails.

## Everglades National Park Trails

*Anhinga.*

Park rangers give hikes, talks, demonstrations and campfire pro- grams during the year. Activities change daily. Ask at the visitor centers for schedules.

**The Anhinga Trail\***, the nearest to the Main Visitor's Center, offers the best opportunity to see several species of wildlife close up. It starts as a paved path, then changes to a raised boardwalk snaking through swamplands past alligators, herons and the namesake anhingas – odd black waterbirds that flatten their wings against the bushes to dry. Other residents include turtles, fish, marsh rabbits and many birds, including herons, egrets, and purple gallinules. Taylor Slough, a freshwater, marshy river, supplies water for this area throughout the dry, winter season. This trail covers less than half a mile.

**The Gumbo Limbo Trail\*** winds one-half mile through a hammock of royal palms, gumbo limbo trees, wild coffee, and lush aerial gardens of ferns and orchids. It starts behind the Royal Palm Visitor's Center, adjacent to the Anhinga Trail.

At **Long Pine Key**, a network of interconnecting trails weave through seven miles of the Pinelands, a wooded refuge for whitetail deer, opossums, raccoons and the endangered Florida panther. Two hundred types of plants, including 30 found nowhere else.

**Shark Valley Trail\*** winds 15 miles through the heart of the Everglades prairie and the headwaters for Shark River. Residents include alligators, otters, wood storks, snakes, deer, wading birds and fish. Shark Valley lies off US 41, the Tamiami Trail. A 50-ft observation tower shadows the Everglades wilderness.

# Sunburn Protection

Avoid prolonged exposure to the sun, especially during peak hours, 10 am to 3 pm. Blistering sunburns are not only painful, they may lead to skin cancer.

• Avoid exposure when taking medicines that i n c r e a s e sunsensitivity.

• Use sunblock lotion or a sunscreen with a protection factor of at least 15.

• Wear sunglasses that block UV rays

• Select hats with a wide brim

• If your activities require prolonged exposure wear protective clothing of fabrics made to block the sun's ultraviolet rays.

The following manufacturers offer catalogues featuring comfortable, protective clothing.

• Sun Precautions Inc., Everett, WA. (800-882-7860).

• Solar Protective Factory, Sacramento, CA. (800-786-2562).

• Koala Konnection, Mountain View, CA.(888-465-6252)

**The Pineland Trail\*** bares the shallow bed of limestone that underlies the area. Less than one-half mile long, it begins near the Main Visitor's Center. Dimples or solution holes and intricate patterns in the exposed limestone erode from deposits of rainwater and organic acid.

**The Pa-hay-okee Overlook Trail**, less than a quarter-mile long, leads to an observation tower where you can view the "river of grass," the true glades that gave the park its name. Sawgrass, Everglades beardgrass, and arrowhead shelter alligators, pygmy rattlesnakes and king snakes. Browse the treetops for red-shouldered hawks and vultures.

**The Mahogany Hammock Trail\***, under half a mile, winds through a cool, fragrant, hardwood hammock of massive mahogany trees, including the largest living specimen in the United

States, and paurotis palms. Look skyward for zebra butterflies, airplants, orchids and huge spider webs that hang from tree branches.

**Snake Bight Trail** leads through just over 1½ miles of tropical hardwood hammock edging Snack Bight Channel. Unpaved, this densely wooded trail offers good bird and alligator watching from the short boardwalk at the path's end.

**Rowdy Bend**, an old road bed, twists through 2½ miles of buttonwood forest and open coastal prairie. It ends at junction with Snake Bight Trail.

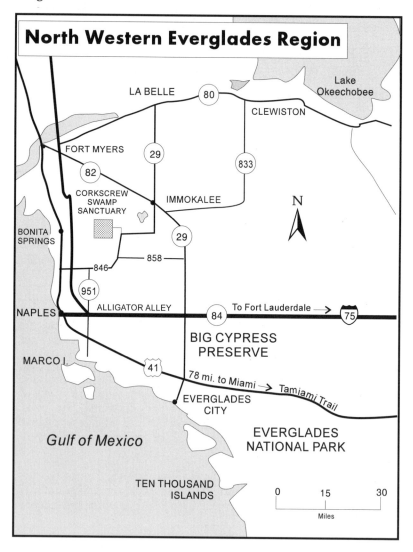

# North Western Everglades Region

Lake Okeechobee

LA BELLE

80

CLEWISTON

FORT MYERS

29

82

CORKSCREW SWAMP SANCTUARY

833

IMMOKALEE

N

BONITA SPRINGS

29

858

846

951

NAPLES

ALLIGATOR ALLEY

84

To Fort Lauderdale →

75

BIG CYPRESS PRESERVE

MARCO I.

41

78 mi. to Miami →

Tamiami Trail

EVERGLADES CITY

Gulf of Mexico

EVERGLADES NATIONAL PARK

TEN THOUSAND ISLANDS

0    15    30

Miles

**Rowdy Bend,** an old road bed, twists through 2½ miles of buttonwood forest and open coastal prairie. It ends at junction with Snake Bight Trail.

**Bear Lake Trail,** an excellent habitat for woodland birds, starts at the Main Park Road and leads through over 1½ miles of dense hardwood hammock to Bear Lake.

**Christian Point,** a short distance from the Flamingo Visitor's Center, is a rustic path that begins in dense buttonwood forest and ends in coastal prairie along the Snake Bight shore.

**Coastal Prairie Trail,** once used by cotton pickers and fishermen, begins at the "C" Loop in the Flamingo Campground, continuing for 7½ miles one way. Park rules require a backcountry permit for camping along this trail.

**Bayshore Loop** zigzags two miles along the shore of Florida Bay, beginning at Coastal Prairie Trailhead behind Loop "C" in the Flamingo Campground. Veer left at the trail junction to the bay.

**Eco Pond,** a half-mile stroll around a freshwater pond, offers a viewing platform from which herons and other wading birds may be photographed.

**Guy Bradley Trail,** parallel to Florida Bay's shoreline, provides a scenic one-mile shortcut between the Flamingo Campground and Visitor's Center. Guy Bradley was a game warden who lost his life defending nesting birds from plume hunters in the late 1800's when egret and heron plumes were in big demand by the millinery industry for decorating ladies' hats.

# Big Cypress

**The Florida Trail,** a well-marked footpath, runs 29 miles across the Big Cypress National Park swamp and pinelands, linking Alligator Alley and the Tamiami Trail. Closed to all vehicles, the trail is primitive. Watch for muck soil, sharp-edged pinnacle rock and holes, as well as poisonous plants and snakes. Two primitive campgrounds on the route offer drinking water. Check with a park ranger before attempting this hike.

For additional information contact: **Big Cypress National Preserve,** Star Route Box 110, Ochopee FL 33943. ☎ 941-695-2000 or 941-262-1066.

# The Corkscrew Swamp Sanctuary

The Corkscrew Swamp Sanctuary sits at the northern tip of what was once the Big Cypress Swamp of Collier County in southwest Florida. The sanctuary, an 11,000-acre wilderness area, contains one of the largest stands of mature bald cypress trees in the nation. Its 2¼-mile boardwalk loop, the most scenic of the Everglades trails, traverses a natural cathedral formed by giant bald cypress trees. Newly built to replace the old boardwalk destroyed by Hurricane Andrew, the walkway now passes through into the best parts of the swamp, including nesting grounds for a woodstork colony, sweet scented sawgrass prairies flanked by ancient forests of slash pine and saw palmetto. Wildlife abounds with basking alligators, flocks of ibis, limpkin (a large dark brown bird that may walk jerkily along or fly off through the trees with a stiff, awkward wingbeat and a peculiar wail), herons, egrets, huge owls, bobcats, otters, the elusive Florida black bear and panther.

Before wandering the well-marked trail, pick up the illustrated self-guiding tour booklet from the park rangers that describes the native plants and animals. Members of the staff are on hand to answer questions and explain the relationships between water, wildlife and man. Gambouzia fish eat the mosquito larvae and eliminate the need for repellent. No pets. The boardwalk is wheel-chair-accessible and wheelchairs are available. Groups may request a naturalist, but should do so in advance.

The sanctuary, located between Naples and Immokalee, sits 1½ miles from County Road 846. The Sanctuary Road entrance (County Road 849) lies 14 miles from Immokalee, 21 miles from Route 41, and 15 miles from Interstate 75, Exit 17. (Note: Do NOT take Exit 19, "Corkscrew Rd" – it won't get you there.) The Visitor's Center and Boardwalk Trail is open from 9 am to 5 pm daily. Admission is $6.50 for adults, $3.00 for a secondary school child. Children under six free. Audubon members $5. For information, write **Corkscrew Swamp Sanctuary**, Route 6, Box 1875-A, Naples Fl 33964. ☎ 941-657-3771.

# Collier Seminole State Park

To reach Collier Seminole State Park, turn off Route 41, the Tamiami Trail (westbound) about 17 miles west of the Route 29 intersection. The 6,423-acre park, named for the late Barron Collier, a pioneer developer in Collier County, and for the Seminole Indians who still live nearby, offers a self-guided hiking trail that winds through 6½ miles of pine flatwood and cypress swamps. A primitive campsite is provided for overnight excursions plus two sites for tent and RV camping.

Artifacts noting the final campaigns of the Second Seminole War are displayed, including a replica of a blockhouse used by US forces and local defenders during that era. One of the "walking dredges" used to build the Tamiami Trail during the 1920's is on exhibit.

There is a boat basin on the Blackwater River, which flows through the park. A canoe trail and rentals available. Handicapped-accessible. For more information contact: **Collier Seminole State Park**, Rt. 4, Box 848, Naples FL 33961. ☎ 914-394-3397.

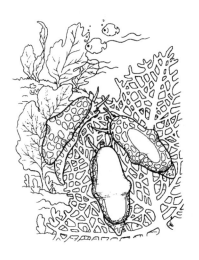

The Curry Mansion Inn

# The Pelican Path

## A Walking Tour of Old Key West

In Key West, you soon forget you are in the United States, as Spanish is heard drifting from porch to porch, while the conchs, the natives of English strain, tell Cockney accented stories of anything from marlins to mermaids. Here, you forget the cares of city life. The sun is always warm, the sky is always clear and just a little way down the street is the most beautiful sea in the world – a pure turquoise color that deepens to emerald on the horizon.

### KEY WEST ARCHITECTURE

The most historic city in South Florida, Key West owes much of its charm to its distinctive architecture. According to the Executive Director of the National Trust for Historic Preservation, "Some of these quaint and charming houses are to be found in no other area of the country." Their history goes back to the time of the first settlers. These pioneers were from the eastern seaboard of the United States, the Bahamas, Cuba and Europe. Many of the old houses in Key West reflect this delightful mixture of nationalities, which has created a special old world atmosphere. The most typical and distinctively Key West style of building is known as

*Material from* The Pelican Path Guide *is reproduced with permission of the Old Island Restoration Foundation, Inc.*

"Conch" or Bahama. Built of wood by ships' carpenters, their simple, clean lines have the balance and grace of a fine sailing ship. They were built to withstand high winds and a tropical climate. Their wide porches have slender square columns that support the main roof. In some instances windows under the eaves open onto the porches. All the windows were protected by shutters or "blinds" that allowed light and air into the high-ceilinged rooms, yet kept out the hot tropic sun. The high peaked roofs were designed to catch the maximum amount of rain water, which was stored in great cisterns. On the small houses, hatches similar to those found on a ship open to allow air and light into the attic bedrooms. The cupolas or "widow's walks" on many of the larger buildings were used as lookouts to scan the nearby reefs for ships that had run aground. These sturdy houses have a classic simplicity, at times relieved by the addition of lacy woodwork or delicately turned spindles on the porch rails.

Nearly all the early buildings were made of wood; however, some were constructed of stone quarried on the island. Two examples are to be seen on Old Mallory Square; others are the Old Stone Methodist Church and the Hemingway House. With the exception of Fort Taylor, brick was not used to any great extent until after the fire of 1886, when half the town was destroyed.

Buildings of various styles, materials and periods can be seen throughout the island. Their architecture is often reminiscent of other places, but somehow there is a difference. In this difference, you will recognize the charm that is found only in "Old Key West."

## THE PELICAN PATH

Colorful Pelican signs mark the route on this unique walking tour of Key West's historic section. Plaques on buildings of special interest are also numbered. Developed by the Old Island Restoration Foundation, it guides you through the quaint older section of the city, teaching about the buildings and their history.

☆ Stars are used to designate historic houses open to the public.

The tour begins at **Hospitality House**, the headquarters of the Old Island Restoration Foundation in Old Mallory Square. Hospitality House was built after the fire of 1886 as the offices for the Southern Express Company. Later, it became the ticket office of the Mallory Steamship Company, which ran coastal steamers between New York, Charleston, Key West and Galveston. The round structures on the seaward side of the house stored cable which was to be laid on the ocean floor for communications with Cuba and the Caribbean. The Hospitality House is now the office of the Old Island Restoration Foundation.

*Follow the arrows on the map to keep on course. Turn right at Pelican 1. Continue to Pelican 2 at the Mallory Square Exit. Continue on Wolfson Lane. Turn right on Front St. at Pelican 3.*

**1 – Harbour House,** 423 Front St. The first Bank of Key West built on this site in 1885 was destroyed by fire the following year. Rebuilt shortly thereafter, the brick building was gutted again by fire in 1984. It is currently being restored. The structure is reminiscent of the architecture found in New Orleans.

**Front Street** was the early commercial district of Key West. Ships from all ports of the world docked here and large warehouses stored goods salvaged from the numerous shipwrecks.

*Cross Whitehead St. to Clinton Place.*

**Clinton Place, Greene and Whitehead Sts.** Within this triangle is a memorial shaft honoring the Union troops who died here during the Civil War, most of whom were victims of Yellow Fever. It was named for DeWitt Clinton, who was the Governor of New York in 1828.

**2 – Coast Guard Building,** Front St. Built in 1856 for a Navy Coaling Station, it was later used in the Civil War as Headquarters for the East Coast Blockade Squadron. As the oldest government building, it is known as "Bldg. 1."

**3 – Old Customs House,** Front St. This ornamental Romanesque brick building was built by the government in 1891 and was used as a Post Office, US Court House and Customs House. The state of Florida has bought the property and the Key West Art & Historical Society is undertaking a multi-year restoration. When completed, it will be the home of the Society's historical museum.

*Continue around Clinton Place, turning right on Whitehead St.*

**4 – ☆ Audubon House (Geiger Home),** 205 Whitehead St. The preservation and restoration of this exceptionally fine old home was responsible for creating a city-wide interest in preserving other buildings of historical and architectural significance. The former home of Captain John H. Geiger, it is now a museum housing an extensive collection of original works by John James Audubon. Period furnishings re-create the era when the naturalist-painter visited the island in 1832. Owned and restored by the Mitchell Wolfson Family Foundation since 1960.

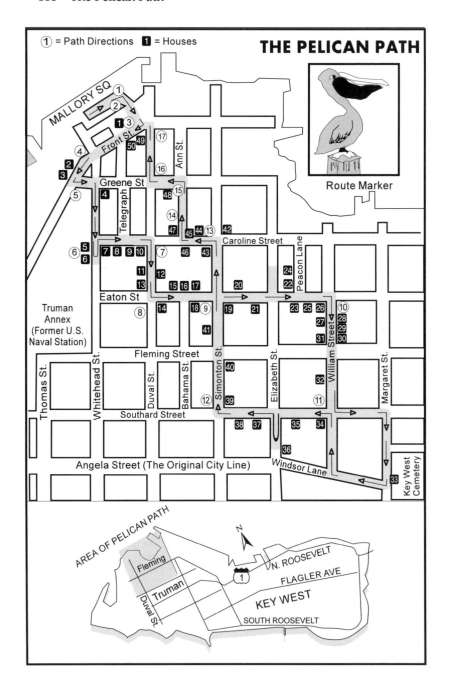

**Whitehead Street**. Of the five military roads built by Commodore David Porter, only this one remains. For many years no other road transversed the full length of the island.

On your right is the **President's Gate**. This ceremonial gate which leads to the "Little White House" museum was opened only for Presidents and other international dignitaries.

**5 – ☆ Harry S. Truman Little White House Museum**, 111 Front Street. Built in 1890 by the Navy as a duplex for the commandant and paymaster. Distinctive wood jalousies shade the porches on three sides. This vacation home of President Truman is now open to the public and is Florida's only presidential home site.

**6 – Navy Houses**, 324, 326 Whitehead. There had been a shortage of suitable officers' housing at the Naval Station from the 1870's and a plan was submitted in 1898 to build Quarters C and D on the 300 block of Whitehead. They are significant as examples of early 20th-century domestic architecture, designed by Navy architects to blend with the surrounding private residences of Key West. In 1905 finishing touches, such as lattice work, porch screens and painting, brought the total cost to $6,000 for both houses. Extensive restoration in 1989 has given these homes new life.

*Turn right on Caroline St.*

**7 – Airways House**, 301 Whitehead St. This building originally stood on the waterfront, where it was used as offices for Aero-Marine Airways. The first international air mail route between Key West and Havana was established November 1, 1920. In October 1927 the route was taken over by Pan American Airways and in January of the following year six passengers made the 90-mile trip in one hour and 20 minutes.

**8 – ☆ Captain George Cary House/Jessie Porter's Heritage House Museum & Robert Frost Cottage**, 410 Caroline St. The original section of this handsome dwelling, built by Captain Carey in 1834, was torn down; however, the old chimney remains and forms a part of the present garden. The existing house was built in the mid-1850's and contains an extensive collection of furnishings, artifacts and mementos from the 1830's to the present day.

**9 – Judge W. Hunt Harris House**, 425 Caroline St. Built toward the end of the Spanish-American War, the building was utilized during that period by the Navy. Judge Harris served in the State Legislature and Senate and was at one time a Lieutenant Governor of Florida.

**10 – J.Y. Porter House**, 429 Caroline St. Dr. J. Y. Porter II was born here in 1847 and died in the same room 80 years later. The Doctor's extensive research in Yellow Fever established our present quarantine laws. In recognition of this, he was made Florida's first Public Health Officer.

*Turn right on Duval St.*

**11 – ☆ Oldest House/Wreckers Museum**, 322 Duval St. Records and deed books indicate that this house was built on Whitehead St. in 1829, then moved to its present location in 1832. It is now owned by the State of Florida and is maintained and managed by the Old Island Restoration Foundation as an operational museum. Of special interest are the three upstairs dormer windows graduating in size and the cook house and garden in the rear.

**12 – Woman's Club**, 319 Duval St. This beautifully proportioned house was built in 1892 by the first manager of the Inter-Ocean Telegraph Office. Since 1941 it has been the home of the Key West Woman's Club.

**13 – Patterson House**, 336 Duval St. Built by Alexander Patterson, it was occupied by Mr. and Mrs. William Pickney and their children. The first private school was conducted here in 1842 by Mrs. Pickney's sister, Mrs. Passalogue, a French lady of rare interests and attainments. The next occupants were the Baldwins, an aristocratic British family who traced their ancestry to Lord Nelson and Sir Robert Walpole.

*Turn left on Eaton St. at Pelican 8.*

**14 – St. Paul's Church**, 401 Duval. This is the oldest Episcopal church in the Diocese of South Florida. The first service was held here on Christmas Day in 1832. The present church, erected in 1916, is the fourth to be built on this site.

**15 – Warren House/Eaton Lodge**, 511 Eaton St. The residence of the Warren family for over 80 years, this home also was the office of Dr. William Richard Warren, an early island physician. It also features the tallest cistern in Key West.

**16 – Skelton House**, 517 Eaton St.

**17 – Alvarez House**, 523 Eaton St. These two lovely homes reflect the unique warmth and ambiance of Old Key West.

**18 – Otto House**, 534 Eaton St. Built by Thomas Osgood Otto, Sr. and completed just before the turn of the century, it is an example of West Indian-Colonial-Victorian architecture and is one of the few remaining homes of this type on the island. The original French wallpaper was mounted on linen so that during a hurricane, if the house rocked, the paper would not crack.

*Cross Simonton St. at Pelican 9.*

**19 – Old Stone Methodist Church**, 600 Eaton St. This handsome church, shaded by a giant Spanish laurel tree, was built in 1877 of stone quarried on the island. It is the oldest religious building in Key West.

**20 – ☆ Peter A. Williams House/Donkey Milk House**, 613 Eaton St. Built in the 1860s and occupied by the same family for over 120 years. US Marshall Williams saved his home from the Great Fire of 1886 by dynamiting along Eaton St. Winner of a 1992 Restoration Award, this unique property is open to the public as a house museum full of delightful furnishings, rare features and quality equipage.

**21 – George H. Curry House**, 620 Eaton St. Built circa 1885, this house is the best example of Greek Revival architecture in Key West. Note the decorative brackets in the architrave and frieze. The large tree in the front is a Canary Island date palm.

**Eaton Street** was named for John Henry Eaton, a United States Senator and later a member of President Andrew Jackson's cabinet. His marriage to Peggy O'Neill created a scandal in Washington. Later, Jackson appointed the controversial Mr. Eaton Governor of Florida.

*Continue on Eaton, crossing Elizabeth St.*

**22 – Saunders House**, 709 Eaton St. Restored in 1975, this pre-Victorian home was first built in 1853 by Eliza and William Uriah Saunders of New Plymouth, Green Turtle Cay in the Bahamas.

**23 – Richard Peacon House**, 712 Eaton St. Richard Peacon, owner of the town's largest grocery store, then at 800 Fleming and now known as William Fleming House, built the house between 1892 and 1899. Often called the "Octagon House," its stark symmetry makes it an architectural standout. Restored and refurbished by the late designer Angelo Donghia, the house was purchased by Calvin Klein in the 1980's for close to $1 million and later re-sold.

**24 – The Susan Peacon House**, 320 Peacon Lane. Peacon Lane was formerly called Grunt Bone Alley. Built about 1848 and lived in by the Peacons for 100 years. Restored in 1972, this small Conch cottage has a well established characteristic Conch garden.

**25 – Filer House**, 724 Eaton St. Built in 1885 and considered one of the classic homes on the island, it is an outstanding example of Bahamian architecture with Victorian influence. Note how the columns are enriched by the ornamental trim.

**26 – Bahama House (I)**, 730 Eaton St. In 1847, John Bartlum and his brother-in-law, Richard Roberts of Green Turtle Cay in the Bahamas, dismantled their homes and brought them to Key West. In 1855 Bartlum built the famous clipper ship *Stephen R. Mallory*. She is said to have been the only clipper ever to be built in Florida.

*Turn right on William St.*

**27 – Bahama House (II)**, 408 William St. This was the home of Richard Roberts, one of the early settlers of the Florida Keys. Unlike any other house on the island, the double verandas extend the entire length of the building. The hand-planed pine siding varies in width and has a unique beading on the lower edges.

**28 – Gideon Lowe House**, 409 William St. The first part of the house was built in the early 1840's and the second section was added in the 1870's. It reflects an outstanding version of Classic Revival architecture.

**29 – Island City House**, 411 William St. Built in the early 1900's, it was operated as a hotel until the late forties. Condemned by the City, it was saved by the present owners and has been handsomely restored.

**30 – Russell House/Key West Bed & Breakfast**, 415 William St. This lovely old house built at the turn of the century exhibits the charm and grace of an earlier age.

**31 – Fleming Street Methodist Church**, 729 Fleming St. The original church was built in 1884 by dissenting members of the mother church who objected to instrumental music. Having been destroyed by the hurricane of 1909, the present concrete structure was completed in 1912. Because many members of the congregation were seamen who wore short jackets, it became known as "the short jacket Methodist church."

*Continue on William St. crossing Fleming St.*

**Fleming Street**. Named for John W.C. Fleming, a native of England and a business partner of John Simonton. Fleming hoped to develop the salt industry here, but his death in 1832 ended the project.

**32 – Charles Roberts House**, 512 Fleming St. Built in the late 1800's, this charming home follows every rule for pleasant island living.

*Turn left on Southard St., then right on Margaret St.*

**33 – Key West Cemetery**. Reminiscent of New Orleans and Galveston graveyards, the unique above-ground vaults are described by Key West poet James Merrill as "whitewashed hope chests." You'll see the *US Maine* monument, a headstone proclaiming "I Told You I Was Sick," chiseled poems, hand-carved angels and glass mausoleums with statuary. Traditional cornet band funeral parades still occur in the cemetery, which was relocated from near the Southernmost Point on Whitehead St. after the devastating 1846 hurricane.

*Turn right on Windsor Lane, then right on William St., then left on Southard St.*

**34 – William Albury House**, 730 Southard St. One of the oldest homes in Key West, it is also considered one of the most interesting. It has double porches on three sides and is crowned with a widow's walk.

**35 – John Albury House**, 708 Southard St. Purchased from the Albury family by Cleveland Dillon in the late 1900's, the house remained in the family until the 1960's.

**36 – Benjamin P. Baker House**, 615 Elizabeth St. Built in 1885, this house is the most elaborate example of the use of decorative gingerbread. This house displayed the strength of structures built by shipwrights when a 1972 tornado knocked it eight feet off its foundation. The house was picked up and put back with no structural damage.

**37 – John Lowe Jr. House**, 620 Southard St. This residence was enlarged as the family and their fortune grew. It is typical of the mid-19th-century homes built by successful Key West merchants, with features that include wide porches and a widow's walk. Mr. Lowe was the owner of one of the largest sponging fleets in Florida.

**38 – Benjamin Curry House**, 610 Southard St. The property was purchased in 1856 from Pardon Greene, who was one of the four original owners of the island. This story-and-a-half house has been the home of six generations of the Curry family.

**39 – William C. Lowe House**, 603 Southard St. Built after 1865, the house remained in the family until 1942. It is of classic design and an outstanding example of restoration.

*Turn left on Simonton St. at Pelican 12.*

**Simonton St.** Named for an American businessman, John W. Simonton, who bought the island of Key West from the Spanish owner Juan Pablo Salas in 1821 for $2,000.

**The Peggy Mills House and Garden**, 516 Angela St. Built prior to 1889, this house was totally renovated in 1982. The gardens, created by Peggy Mills, furniture store owner and plant lover, were started in 1930, and for 50 years Peggy never stopped adding to them. Internationally known for its varied botanical collection, the gardens also feature antique tinajones (Cuban water jugs weighing one ton empty) and winding pathways of century-old brick.

*Return to Southard St. turn left, then right on Duval St. Turn right on Fleming St.*

**40 – John Haskins Building/Marquesa Hotel**, 600 Fleming. Built prior to 1889, this structure is now a small luxury hotel which was the 1988 First Place Winner for Historic Preservation. It has been a drugstore, car dealership and the first home of Fausto's grocery, now located in the next block.

**41 – William R. Kerr House**, 410 Simonton St. Built in 1876 by the owner, the house shows the strong influence of Downings' Carpenter Gothic design in the roof style, verge boards and porch ornaments. Mr. Kerr, a prominent architect, built many of the important public structures on the island.

**42 – Richard Kemp/Cypress House**, 601 Caroline St. An excellent example of Bahamian architecture in its purest form. Its simplicity of lines and styling with fine proportions and balance reflect the craftsmanship of ships' carpenters. The Kemp family migrated from the Bahamas to Key West shortly after the island was settled. William Kemp introduced the sponge industry to Key West and sold the first shipment of Florida sponges in New York.

*Turn left on to Caroline St*

**43 – Delaney House**, 532 Caroline St. Built around 1889, it was owned by John J. Delaney, a merchant in the clothing business. This handsome structure has been used for various business and professional offices but has retained its original architecture.

**44 – George Bartlum House**, 531 Caroline St. Built in the mid-1800's in three stages, it was finished in 1888. President and Mrs. Harry Truman were frequent guests in this home.

**45 – Bott House**, 529 Caroline St. This distinctive house is one of the few brick homes in Key West.

**46 – George B. Patterson House**, 522 Caroline St. Mr. Patterson's father, Col. Alexander Patterson, came to Key West from Connecticut in the 1820's. The design of the house reflects the Queen Anne style of architecture.

*Turn right on Ann St.*

**47 – ☆ Milton Curry House/Curry Mansion Inn**, 511 Caroline St. Built in 1905, this house is a copy of a Newport cottage that the young couple had admired. A wide graceful porch surrounds the house on three sides. Of special interest is the elegant design and detail on the verandas and under the eaves.

**48 – Old City Hall**, 512 Greene St. Built in 1891 on the same site as the former City Hall destroyed in the 1886 fire. This historic landmark is presently being restored by the Historic Florida Keys Preservation Board, Old Island Restoration Foundation, the City of Key West and its generous citizens.

*Turn left on Greene St. Turn right on Duval St.*

**Duval St.** has for many years been the city's main shopping and entertainment center. It was named for Florida's first Territorial Governor, William Pope Duval.

**49 – Florida First National Bank**, Front and Duval Sts. This establishment has been in operation since 1891. The original building shows strong Spanish influence in the beautiful and intricate brick work as well as in the ornate balcony. On display in the lobby is part of the famous solid gold table service made by Tiffany.

*Turn left on Front St.*

**50 – Sawyer Building**, 400 Front St. Erected after the fire of 1886 by a Bahamian merchant. It is one of the many structures built during this era by immigrant Irish brick layers from Boston. The second floor was at one time used by the US District Court.

# Parasailing

Parasailing combines the thrill of hang gliding with the excitement of parachuting. It's much safer, requires no training and you don't need to jump out of an airplane or from a towering cliff. The new custom parasailing boats allow you to take off and land right on the deck.

Once you buy your ticket and climb aboard, the boat moves to an open, over-water area. Next you are strapped into a life jacket and special harness. The deck hand slackens your safety line and, within seconds, you are whisked 400 feet aloft. The ride lasts about 15 minutes. As the powerboat pulls you across a panorama of coral reefs, mangrove islands and coves, you ride a column of air and see the world from a birdseye view. Like a kite, you are always connected to the boat by a safety line. Light wind and calm sea conditions are necessary.

As long as the boat is moving, the relative wind keeps you up. When you wish to come down, the boat slows up. You settle toward earth and are reeled back aboard the boat by an electric winch. Photo and video opportunities are magnificent.

Don't worry if the boat runs out of gas and the winch motor breaks. That big nylon apparatus you are hanging from is a parachute. If all fails, you will float gently down and splash into the sea.

Wear a bathing suit. When you parasail with **Joe Roth at Holiday Isle**, getting wet is part of the fun. His custom-designed parasail boat is kept in tip-top shape, but his patrons demand an intentional dip in the sea to cool off. After 15 minutes close to Florida's sun you'll want one too. You can sign up for a trip with Joe on the Holiday Isle beach at **Mojo's Shack** (☎ 664-5390) or at the huge "parasailing" sign on the north end of the beach. Six people can go in the boat at once. Spectators ride along for a nominal fee. A special tandem parasail set-up allows a parent to take a small child along. A new tandem harness allows for side-by-side seating. Arrangements for the handicapped are available. A new 1,000-ft flight has been recently added.

In Key Largo you can lift off at **Caribbean Watersports** on the beach at the Sheraton (☎ 305-852-4707). Caribbean Watersports at Cheeca Lodge, ☎ 305-664-4651, MM 82, offers parasailing as well. **Parawest Parasailing Adventures** departs from the foot of Front St., Key West (☎ 305-292-5199).

# Scuba

Spectacular coral reefs, offshore from Florida's Keys, attract nearly a million sport divers each year. Patches of finger-like spur and groove reefs parallel the islands from Key Biscayne to Key West and are inhabited by over 500 varieties of fish and corals. Shallow depths, ideal for underwater video and still photography, range from just below the surface to an average maximum of 40 feet.

## Getting Ready

A scuba certification card (C-card) is required to join dive boat trips or obtain air fills. Dive operators may request a look at your logbook before signing you on a trip. Without one, you may be asked to take a check-out dive. An advanced scuba certification is

*Wreck dive.*

required for dives on the deep wrecks, *Duane* and *Bibb*. Many dive shops offer resort courses. You take a lesson in a pool, then an introductory dive on a shallow reef with an instructor. Refresher courses are available too.

## GEAR

During winter, air and ocean temperatures average 70-75°F. Topside temperatures may drop as low as 40°F. Plan on wearing either a shorty or one-eighth full wetsuit. A quarter-inch wetsuit is not uncomfortable once in the water.

During summer, water temperatures climb to 85°F, making a wetsuit unnecessary. A safe-second regulator is encouraged, but not mandatory. Standard gear – bouyancy compensators, weight belts, weights, mask, knife, snorkel, camera and video equipment – may be rented at dive shops. Boaters will find small craft for rent at the marinas.

## WEATHER

Good diving on the Florida Keys shallow reefs (most 45 ft or less) depends on good weather conditions. High winds that churn up surface swells also stir up the sandy bottom. You might plan a dive the morning after a storm and find visibility as low as 25 ft, yet return in the afternoon to calm seas and visibility in excess of 100 ft. October through June offer the best weather conditions. Because the reefs are fairly shallow, winds that churn up the seas may cause lowered visibility.

When storms rule out trips to the outer reefs, visit the Content Keys, a sheltered area on the Gulf side of Marathon that is almost always calm.

## CEDAM

Specialized study programs and unique scientific expeditions, such as collecting artifacts from ancient shipwrecks for museums or mapping underwater terrain, are offered by CEDAM, a non-profit organization. For information on Florida Keys trips, call or write: CEDAM International, Fox Road, Croton-on-Hudson NY 10520. ☎ 914-271-5365.

# The Florida Keys National Marine Sanctuary

After three freighters grounded on the reefs in 1989, destroying acres of the tiny coral reef organisms, President Bush signed into law a bill designed to protect a 3,000-square-mile stretch of Florida Keys land and sea. The area known as The Florida Keys National Marine Sanctuary contains the entire strand of Keys barrier reefs on the Atlantic and Gulf sides of the islands. Freighter traffic close to shore is prohibited, providing a safe "cushion" area between keels and corals.

The sanctuary, managed by the National Oceanographic and Atmospheric Administration, also encompasses, and dwarfs, two previous federal preserves in the Keys, the Looe Key National Marine Sanctuary and the Key Largo National Marine Sanctuary. In contrast to the new 3,500-square-mile sanctuary, the Looe Key sanctuary is 5.32 square miles and the Key Largo sanctuary is 100 square miles. Within the sanctuary, spearfishing, wearing gloves and anchoring on the coral are prohibited.

On the ocean reefs, replenishment reserves are being set up to protect and enhance the spawning, nursery or permanent resident areas of fish and other marine life. Some areas will restrict fishing, will allow diving, but will be "no-take" areas. Prime areas are shallow, heavily used reefs. Check with local dive or bait shops for current information before diving on your own.

# Biscayne National Park Marine Sanctuary

Biscayne National Park Marine Sanctuary is gaining interest from those who enjoy uncrowded dive spots. This is thanks to a long struggle by Vietnam veteran and Audubon activist, Ed Davidson. He masterminded a successful fight to save this Northern Key Largo area from development.

Diving in Biscayne is relatively new, with many virgin areas waiting to be discovered. Pristine reefs are the norm, though some of the shallow reefs were damaged during Hurricane Andrew. Major

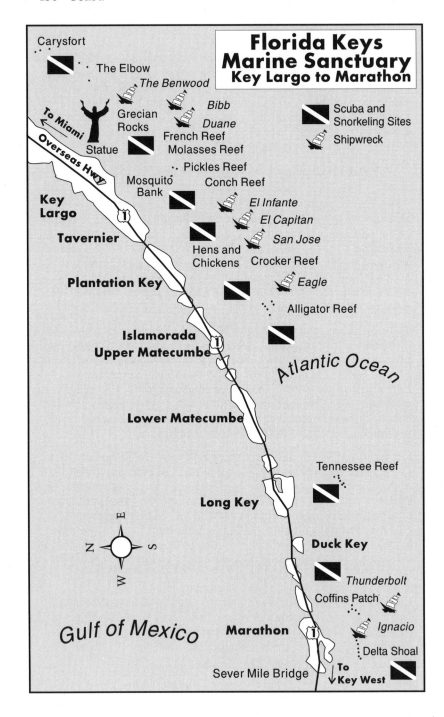

Carysfort
The Elbow
The Benwood
Grecian Rocks
Bibb
Duane
French Reef
Molasses Reef
Statue

**Florida Keys Marine Sanctuary**
Key Largo to Marathon

Scuba and Snorkeling Sites
Shipwreck

To Miami
Overseas Hwy

Key Largo
Tavernier

Pickles Reef
Mosquito Bank
Conch Reef
El Infante
El Capitan
San Jose
Hens and Chickens
Crocker Reef

Plantation Key

Eagle
Alligator Reef

Islamorada
Upper Matecumbe

Atlantic Ocean

Lower Matecumbe

Tennessee Reef

Long Key

N E S W

Duck Key

Thunderbolt
Coffins Patch
Ignacio
Delta Shoal

Gulf of Mexico

Marathon

Sever Mile Bridge

To Key West

# Florida Keys Marine Sanctuary
## Bahia Honda to Key West

Scuba and Snorkeling Sites

Shipwreck

Content Keys

Sugarloaf

Alexander's Wreck

Ramrod Key

Summerland

Bahia Honda

Key West   Maryland Shoal

Sambos

Dry Rocks

American Shoal

Looe Key   Big Pine Shoal

Rock Key

Sand Key

Aquanaut

U.S.S. Wilkes Barre

coral reef patches lie two to three miles offshore and require a boat for access. Dive and snorkeling tours take off from Convoy Point, nine mile east of Homestead (☎ 305-230-1100).

# John Pennekamp Coral Reef State Park

John Pennekamp Coral Reef State Park has long been the most popular diving area in Florida. John D. Pennekamp (1897-1978), editor of the *Miami Herald*, fostered the idea of reef preservation and, with fellow ecologists, raised enough money to purchase the southwest edge of Largo Sound for a headquarters site. The park, part of the Florida Keys National Marine Sanctuary, consists of 100 square miles of undersea reefs and 75 land acres as a haven not only for divers and snorkelers, but also campers, bird watchers, fishermen and sunbathers.

Before the area attained park status in 1960, corals and conch shells were harvested and bleached for souvenirs, while spear fishermen killed angelfish and anything else that moved underwater. Today, concern continues as environmentalists fight overdevelopment and accompanying ocean pollutants.

## DESILT SPONGES & CORALS

To breathe and eat, sponges must be able to suck in water for oxygen and nutrients. Wave action cleanses them of most natural silting, but they have no mechanism to rid themselves of silt kicked up by divers and snorkelers.

If you see a silt-covered sponge or coral, give it a hand by fanning the surrounding water to "blow" off the residue.

*Courtesy of Dee Scarr.*

## Scuba Tours

Dive shop signs and billboards offering reef trips line the highway throughout Key Largo. Boat trips to the best dive sites takes from 15-30 minutes depending on sea and wind conditions.

## Dive Sites

The park's most popular dive, underwater wedding site and perhaps the one that symbolizes the area, is "the statue," a nine-ft bronze replica of **"Christ of the Abyss,"** created by sculptor Guido Galletti for placement in the Mediterranean Sea. The statue was given to the Underwater Society of America in 1961 by industrialist Egidi Cressi.

The top of the statue is in 10 ft of water and can be seen easily from the surface. The base rests on a sandy bottom, 20 ft down, and is surrounded by huge brain corals and elkhorn formations. Stingrays and barracuda inhabit the site. A buoy marks the statue's location, but small swells make it difficult to pinpoint. If you are unfamiliar with navigating in the park, join one of the commercial dive trips. Extreme shallows in the area provide outstanding snorkeling areas, but make running aground a threat.

More easily found is **Molasses Reef**, marked by a huge, lighted steel tower in the southeast corner of the park. Noted as the area's most popular reef dive, it carries the distinction of having had two shiploads of molasses run aground on its shallows.

The reef provides several dives, depending on where your boat is moored. Moorings M21 through M23 are for diving. M1 through M20 are shallow and better for snorkeling.

High-profile coral ridges form the perimeter of a series of coral ridges, grooves, overhangs, ledges and swim-through tunnels. In one area, divers see huge silver tarpon, walls of grunts, snappers, squirrel fish and Spanish hogfish. In another, divers swim over an ancient Spanish anchor. Visibility often exceeds 100 ft.

Be sure to check the current at Molasses before entering the water, since an occasional strong flow makes the area undiveable. Depths vary from very shallow to approximately 40 ft.

## BAILOUT A CRAB

**ECO TIP**

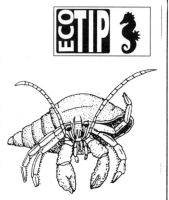

Plastic materials are often smoother than some ocean animals' feet were meant to walk on. Plastic buckets lying mouth up on the sea floor wreak havoc with hermit crabs, who crawl in, then can't get out. They eat the bottom ring of algae, then slowly starve to death.

When you see a new bucket or container on the sea floor, simply bring it back up to the surface and dispose of it properly. If the bucket is coral-encrusted on the outside, leave it, but put a pile of debris or coral rubble inside to form a ramp out for wandering crabs. If no rubble is at hand, cut an escape hole in the bottom or side with your dive knife or shears. Take care not to handle any coral directly or you may get a nasty infection.

*Courtesy of Dee Scarr.*

Slightly northeast of Molasses stands **French Reef**, an area many consider the prettiest in the park, with swim-through tunnels, caves, and ledges carpeted in pink and lavender sea fans, tube sponges, soft corals and anemones. Shallow depths range from areas where the reef pierces the surface to 45 ft.

North of French Reef lies the wreck of the *Benwood*, a 300-ft freighter hit by a German submarine during World War II and later sunk as a navigational hazard by the Coast Guard.

Presently under guard by throngs of sergeant majors, grunts, and yellowtails, the wreck sits on a sandy bottom at 45 ft. Lobsters, huge morays and stingrays peek out from beneath the hull as huge groupers and turtles blast by. During summer, swirls of glass minnows hover about the wreck.

Despite pristine reefs and a robust fish population, a long boat ride prevents most dive operators from frequenting **Carysfort Reef**, located in the northeast corner of the park.

If you are fortunate enough to catch a trip out there, expect a good display of fish and the possibility of one huge, resident barracuda, tamed by a local divemaster, swimming up to within an inch of your mask. This unique, engaging plea for a handout makes the toothy guy tough to ignore. But sanctuary officials greatly discourage fish feeding so try to resist sharing your lunch.

Instead, explore the reef's healthy display of staghorn, elkhorn and star corals at depths varying from very shallow to 65 ft. Normally calm waters make Carysfort a good choice for novice and experienced divers, but beware the dramatic overhangs that top the walls. We discovered some the hard way – by surfacing without first looking up.

Just south of Carysfort Reef lies **The Elbow**, a crescent-shaped spur-and-groove reef littered with the twisted remains of two steamers – The *City of Washington*, and The *Tonawanda*. Near the wrecks lie ballast and the frail remains of a wooden ship known as *The Civil War Wreck*. Depths average 40 feet. Visibility is usually good, with an occasional strong current. Friendly barracuda and tame moray eels await.

## Key Largo's Artificial Reef

In November, 1987, two vintage Coast Guard cutters were sunk off Key Largo by a team of Navy divers. The 1930's-era sister cutters *Bibb* and *Duane* whose careers took them from the Caribbean and

Cap Cod and included duties in the North Atlantic, Pacific and Mediterranean, were towed to their final resting site following cleaning and removal of potential hazards for divers.

The *Bibb* sits on her side in 125 ft of water, while the *Duane* sits upright at 130 ft. The top of the *Duane* can be viewed at 75 ft. They rest seven miles offshore and one mile south of Molasses Reef. This area is a buffer zone around the Key Largo National Marine Sanctuary. Both ships have attracted huge grouper, schooling tropicals, barracuda, eels and rays. An occasional hammerhead or nurse shark makes an appearance.

The ships, now camouflaged with a thin layer of coral, were part of a seven-vessel "Secretary" class built by the Coast Guard in the late 1930s, with their original role as long-range rescue ships, according to Dr. Robert Scheina, a Coast Guard historian. "The vessels were also built to prevent poaching by Japanese fishing vessels in Alaskan Waters and a third purpose – one quite familiar to today's Coast Guard. There was a problem with opium smuggling from the Orient to various outlets on the west coast of the United States. The vessels were utilized for drug interdiction back then."

With spare parts for the *Bibb* and *Duane* difficult to obtain and with excessive maintenance costs, the Coast Guard de-commissioned the ships in 1985 and turned them over to the United States Maritime Administration for disposal.

*The Statue, Key Largo.*

*Wreck of the* Duane.

South of Pennekamp Park lies **Pickles Reef**, a shallow area rich with marine life, sea fans and boulder corals. Near Pickles is **Conch Reef**, a wall dive that drops off to more than 100 ft, and the wreck of the *Eagle*, a 287-ft freighter sunk intentionally to create an artificial reef. Residents of the wreck include parrot fish, schools of grunts, sergeant majors, moray eels and angels.

Another popular site frequented by Islamorada dive shops is **Alligator Reef**, home to walls of grunts, parrotfish and groupers and an occasional nurse shark. There are some nice stands of elkhorn and brain corals.

More spectacular, though, are the reefs surrounding the Marquesas Islands, 30 miles from Key West, and the Dry Tortugas, 70 miles off Key West.

# REEF ETIQUETTE

Do not allow your hands, knees, tank or fins to contact the coral. Touching coral causes damage to the fragile polyps.

Spearfishing in the sanctuary is not allowed. This is one reason the fish are so friendly that you can almost reach out and touch them.

Hand feeding of fish is discouraged, especially food unnatural to them. Besides the risk of bodily injury, such activity changes the natural behavior of the fish.

Hook and line fishing is allowed. Applicable size, catch limits and seasons must be observed.

Spiny lobster may be captured during the season except in the Core Area of the Looe Key Sanctuary. Number and size regulations must be followed.

Corals, shells, starfish and other animals cannot be removed from the Sanctuary.

Regulations prohibiting littering and discharge of any substances except chum are strictly enforced.

Fines are imposed for running aground or damaging coral. Historical artifacts are protected.

The red and white dive flag must be flown while diving or snorkeling. Boats must go slow enough to leave no wake within 100 yards of a dive flag.

# Diving The Middle Keys

Dive sites in the Middle Keys – from Long Key Bridge to the Seven Mile Bridge – are similar to, but often less crowded than those in Key Largo. Besides the offshore reefs and wrecks, the Marathon area has a number of sunken vessels around the new and old bridges that serve as artificial reefs for fishing. When currents are mild, you can dive a few of these spots; they abound with fish, sponges and soft corals.

**Sombrero Reef**, Marathon's most popular ocean dive and snorkeling spot, offers good visibility and a wide depth range from the shallows to 40 feet. Cracks and crevices shot through the coral

*John Pennekamp Coral Reef State Park, Key Largo.*

canyons that comprise the reef overflow with lobster, arrow crabs, octopi, anemones, and resident fish. A huge light tower marks the area. Boaters must tie up to the mooring bouys on the reef.

Slightly north of Sombrero lies the wreck of the *Thunderbolt*, an intentionally scuttled, 188-ft freighter lying upright in 110 ft of water with the top of its wheelhouse at 70 ft. Resident fish include big barracuda, swarms of sergeant majors, queen and grey angelfish, blue tangs and moray eels.

**Coffins Patch**, just north of the *Thunderbolt*, provides good snorkeling areas with mounds of pillar, elkhorn, and brain corals at depths averaging 20-30 ft.

# Diving The Lower Keys & Key West

Dive trips from The Lower Keys – Big Pine Key, Sugar Loaf Key, Summerland Key, Ramrod Key, Cudjoe Key and Torch Key, take off to reefs surrounding **American Shoal** and **Looe Key National Marine Sanctuary**.

The **Looe Key** reef tract, named for the *HMS Looe*, a British frigate that ran aground on the shallow reefs in 1744, offers vibrant elkhorn and staghorn coral thickets, an abundance of sponges, soft corals and fish. Constant residents include Cuban hogfish, queen parrotfish, huge barracuda, and longsnout butterfly fish. A favorite dive site of the Lower Keys, Looe Key bottoms out at 35 feet. Extreme shallow patches of seagrass and coral rubble provide a calm habitat for juvenile fish and invertebrates.

Diving off Key West includes offshore wreck dives and tours of **Cotrell Key, Sand Key** and the **Western Dry Marks**. Huge pelagic fish and graceful rays lure divers to this area.

**Sand Key**, marked by a lighthouse, lures snorkelers and novice divers to explore its fields of staghorn coral. Depths range from the surface down to 45 ft.

**Cosgrove Reef**, noted for its large heads of boulder and brain coral, attracts a number of large fish and rays.

Advanced divers may want to tour the *Cayman Salvage Master* at 90 feet. This 180-ft vessel was purposely sunk to form an artificial reef.

Seldom visited, though pristine for diving, are the Marquesas Islands, 30 miles off Key West. Extreme shallows both enroute and surrounding the islands make the boat trip difficult in all but the calmest seas and docking impossible for all but shallow-draft cats and trimarans. Check with **Lost Reef Adventures** (☎ 305-296-9737) for trip availability.

## DRY TORTUGAS

Seventy miles to the west are the Dry Tortugas, where the most fabulous diving in the Keys can be found. No services though. You reach the area by charter boat or seaplane (☎ 305-294-6978) and should carry in all of your gear and air. Check with Key West dive shops for the availability of trips (see also Aerial Tours chapter). For the very adventurous, overnight camping trips can be arranged.

# Dive Operators

The following operators provide guided reef and wreck trips. Many also arrange complete dive and accommodation packages.

## KEY LARGO

**Abyss Eco Charters**
MM 100
Key Largo FL 33037
☎ 305-451-6030

**Admiral Dive**
MM 103.2
Key Largo FL 33037
☎ 800-346-3483 or 305-451-1114

**American Diving Headquarters**
MM 105.5, Bayside
Key Largo FL 33037
☎ 305-451-0037

**Amy Slate's Amoray Dive Center, Inc.**
104250 Overseas Highway
MM 104, Bayside
Key Largo FL 33037
☎ 305-451-3595, 305-451-4645
800-426-6729 or 800-4-A-MORAY

**Adventure Watersports Inc**
MM 104
Key Largo FL 33037
☎ 305-451-3009

**Absolute Dive Charters**
MM 104
Key Largo FL 33037
☎ 305-453-9405

**Aqua-Nuts**
(At Kelly's on the Bay)
103750 Overseas Hwy
MM103, Bayside
Key Largo FL 33037
☎ 800-226-0415 or 305-451-1622

**Atlantis Dive Center, Inc.**
51 Garden Cove Dr.
MM 106.5, Oceanside
Key Largo FL 33037
☎ 305-451-1325 or 305-451-3020

**Captain Corky's Diver's World**
MM 99.5
Key Largo FL 33037
☎ 800-445-8231 or 305-451-3200

**Conch Republic Divers, Inc.**
90311 Overseas Highway
Tavenier FL 33070
☎ 800-274-DIVE or 305-852-1655

**Discovery Dive**
MM 101.5
Key Largo FL 33037
☎ 305-453-9630

**Dive Shop at Ocean Reef Club**
10 Fishing Village Dr
North Key Largo FL 33037
☎ 305-367-3051

**Divers City USA**
MM 104, Oceanside
Key Largo FL 33037
☎ 305-451-4554

**Divers Outlet Store**
MM 106, Bayside
Key Largo FL 33037
☎ 305-451-0815

**Floridaze Dive Center**
MM 90.8
Tavernier Creek Marina
Tavernier FL 33070
☎ 305-852-1432

**HMS Minnow Charters Inc**
MM 100, Oceanside
Holiday Inn Docks
Key Largo FL 33037
☎ 800-366-9301, 451-7834

**Island Bay Resort**
MM 92.5, Bayside
Tavernier FL 33070
☎ 305-852-4087

**Island Ventures**
Rowell's Marina
MM 104.5
Key Largo FL 33037
☎ 305-451-4957

**Florida Keys Dive Center**
90500 Overseas Hwy, MM 90.5
Plantation Key FL 33070
☎ 305-852-4599

**Stephen Frink Photographic**
MM 102, Bayside
Key Largo FL 33037
☎ 800-451-3737 or 305-451-3737

**Lady Go Dive Charters**
MM 92
Tavernier FL 33070
☎ 305-852-0839

**Ocean Divers, Inc**
522 Caribbean Dr., MM 100
Key Largo FL 33037
☎ 305-451-1113

**Pennekamp State Park
Dive Center**
Located at John Pennekamp Park
or ☎ 305-451-1621

**Pisces Aquatics**
MM 94.5 Oceanside
Key Largo, FL 33037
☎ 305-852-5626 or 800-852-3756

**Quiescence Diving Service**
MM 103.5, Key Largo FL 33037
☎ 305-451-2440

**Reef Divers**
MM 100, Oceanside at Ocean Bay
Marina
Key Largo FL 33037
☎ 305-451-3109

**Sea Dwellers Sports Center**
99850 Overseas Hwy, MM 100
Key Largo FL 33037
☎ 305-451-3640

**Sharkey's Inc.**
MM 106 Plaza
☎ 305-451-5533
MM 106 Dive Ctr.
☎ 305-451-3711
Key Largo FL 33037

**Silent World Dive Center, Inc.**
P.O. Box 2363, MM 103.2
Key Largo FL 33037
☎ 800-966-DIVE or 305-451-3252

**Tavernier Dive Center**
MM 90.7
Tavernier FL 33070
☎ 800-537-3253 or 305-852-4007

**Trident Divers**
MM 100, Holiday Inn Docks
Key Largo FL 33037
☎ 305-451-6431

**Tropic Vista Motel
& Dive Shop**
MM 90.5, Oceanside
Plantation Key FL 33037
☎ 305-853-0526

**Tropical Descent**
107900 Overseas Highway
Key Largo FL 33037
☎ 305-451-1141

**Upper Keys Dive
& Sports Center**
MM 90.7, Oceanside
Plantation Key FL 33070
☎ 305-853-0526

## ISLAMORADA

**Ambassador Diving
& Boat Rental**
MM 90.5, Plantation Key
Islamorada FL 33036
☎ 305-853-0222

**Bud 'n Mary's Dive Center**
MM 80, Islamorada FL 33036
☎ 305-664-2211

**Cheeca Divers at Cheeca Lodge**
MM 82 Islamorada FL 33036
☎ 800-934-8377 or 305-664-2777

**Holiday Isle Dive Shop**
P.O. Box 482
Islamorada FL 33036
☎ 800-327-7070 or 305-664-4145

**Lady Cyana Divers**
MM 85.9
Islamorada FL 33036
☎ 800-221-8717 or 305-664-8717

**Ocean Quest Dive Center**
87000 Overseas Hwy.
MM 87
Islamorada FL 33036
☎ 800-356-8798 or 305-852-8770

**Rainbow Reef Dive Center**
MM 85, Oceanside
Islamorada FL 33036
☎ 305-664-4600

**Reef Shop Dive Center**
84771 Overseas Hwy., MM 84.7
Islamorada FL 33036
☎ 305-664-4385

**Upper Keys Dive
& Sports Center**
MM 90.7
Plantation Key FL 33070
☎ 305-853-0526

**World Down Under**
MM 81.5, Islamorada FL 33036
☎ 305-664-9312, FL 800-245-DIVE

## MARATHON

**Abyss Pro Dive Center**
13175 Overseas Highway
(Behind the Holiday Inn at MM 54)
Marathon FL 33050
☎ 800-457-0134 or 305-743-2126

**Abyss Pro Dive Center**
Hawk's Cay Resort, MM 61
Marathon FL 33050
☎ 800-432-2242 or 305-289-4433

**CJ's Dive Center**
MM 48.5, Marathon FL 33050
☎ 305-289-9433

**Camelot Divers**
1200 Ocean View Ave
Marathon FL 33050
☎ 305-743-9369

**Captain Hook's Dive Center**
11833 Overseas Highway
Marathon FL 33050
☎ 305-743-2444

**The Diving Site**
MM 53.5, Marathon FL 33050
☎ 305-289-1021

**Hall's Diving Center**
1994 Overseas Hwy
Marathon FL 33050
☎ 800-331-4255 or 305-743-2902

**Hawk's Cay Resort & Marina**
MM 61, Duck Key
Marathon FL 33050
☎ 305-743-7000

**Ocean Adventures**
Hawk's Cay Marina
☎ 800-331-HALL or 305-743-5929

**Hurricane Aqua-Center**
10800 Overseas Hwy
Marathon FL 33050
☎ 305-743-2400

**Marathon Divers**
MM 53.5
Marathon FL 33050
☎ 305-289-1141

**Marathon Undersea Adventures**
MM 48.5 (Buccaneer Resort)
Marathon FL 33050
☎ 305-743-9867

**Middle Keys Scuba Center**
11511 Overseas Highway
Marathon FL 33050
☎ 305-743-2902

**Rick's Watercraft Rentals**
4590 Overseas Highway
Marathon FL 33050
☎ 305-743-2450

**Tilden's Pro Dive Shop**
MM 49.5
Marathon FL 33050
☎ 800-223-4563 or 305-743-5422

## BIG PINE & THE LOWER KEYS

**Cudjoe Gardens Marina & Dive Center**
MM 21 (Turn at Sheriff's Substation)
Cudjoe Key FL 33042
☎ 305-745-2357

**Innerspace Dive Shop**
MM 29.5, Big Pine Key FL 33043
☎ 305-872-2319

**Reef Runner Dive Shop**
MM 25, Summerland Key FL 33042
☎ 305-745-1549

**Underseas, Inc.**
MM 30.5, Big Pine Key FL 33043
☎ 800-446-5663 or 305-872-2700

**Scuba Concepts**
Pirates Road
Little Torch Key FL 33043
☎ 305-872-9766

## KEY WEST

**A Key West Reef Trip**
Dive tours on a 65-ft sailing
schooner; ☎ 305-292-1345

**Adventure Charters**
Dive from a 42-ft Trimaran
6810 Front St
Stock Island FL 33040
☎ 305-296-0362

**Ahoy Hurricane Bill Says**
430 Greene St.
Key West FL 33040
☎ 305-292-2042

**Beachside Watersports**
**& Holiday Divers of Key West**
3841 N Roosevelt Blvd
Key West FL 33040
☎ 305-294-5934

**Bob Holston's Key West**
**Pro Dive Shop**
3128 N. Roosevelt Blvd
Key West FL 33040
☎ 305-296-3823

**Bonsai Diving**
310 Duval Street
Key West FL 33040
☎ 305-294-2921
(after hours 305-296-6301)

**Captain Billy's**
**Key West Diver, Inc.**
MM 4.5
Stock Island FL 33040
☎ 305-294-7177

**Captain'S Corner Dive Center**
Ocean Key House Hotel
O Duval Street
Key West FL 33040
☎ 305-296-8865; 800-328-9815

**Looker Diving Center**
100 Grinnell Street
Key West FL 33040
☎ 305-294-2249

**Lost Reef Adventures**
261 Margaret St.
At Lands End Village
Key West FL 33040
☎ 800-633-6833 or 305-296-9737

**Reef Raiders Dive Shop**
617 Front St.
Key West FL 33040
☎ 305-294-0660 or 305-294-3635

**Rock & Reel**
Dive/fishing tours
Specializing in 17th- and
18th-century wrecks
☎ 305-745-8999

**Seaclypse Divers**
6000 Peninsula Av.
Key West FL 33040
☎ 305-296-1975

**Southpoint Divers**
714 Duval St.
Key West FL 33040
☎ 305-296-9914

**Subtropic Dive Center**
1605 N Roosevelt Blvd
Key West FL 33040
☎ 305-296-9914

**Tilden's Booth**
222 Duval St.
2319 N. Roosevelt Blvd.
Key West FL 33040
☎ 800-370-7745 or 305-292-7745

# Snorkeling

If you can swim, you'll love snorkeling. Florida Keys offshore reefs offer endless entertainment to anyone who can peer through a mask. There are shallow shipwrecks, such as the wreck of the *San Pedro*, an underwater archaeological preserve off Islamorada, miles of coral canyons and pinnacles, the famous Statue of Christ in Key Largo, and every imaginable fish along the entire coast.

The best spots to snorkel are the outer reefs. Morning and afternoon boat trips are widely available. If given a choice, select the morning trips, which are less crowded, with usually calmer wind and seas. Take a snorkeling lesson if you're new to the sport. A short pool demonstration will allow you to get comfortable using the gear before you try it in the ocean. Many hotels and dive shops offer classes.

If high winds or storms cancel ocean tours, you can still explore the bays or oceanside lagoons (dive shops will rent you the gear). We found a number of juvenile barracuda, parrot fish, filefish, angels and grunts around the bayside hotel docks and swimming lagoons. Just off the beach at John Pennekamp State Park are some old cannons and a sunken car. This artificial reef attracts numerous fish and crustaceans. An occasional manatee has been spotted there too.

For a fee, you can snorkel over the first underwater hotel – Jules' Undersea Lodge located in the **Key Largo Undersea Park**. The park is a protected lagoon and open 365 days a year. Though the fish and visibility do not rival the offshore reefs, this is a good spot for beginners or when storms rule out ocean tours. To reach the lagoon, turn toward the ocean at the "Undersea Park" sign (MM 103.2). The lagoon is at the end of the road.

# Places To Avoid

Snorkeling is unsafe in the brackish and fresh waters of the Everglades – home to alligators. There is a crocodile sanctuary on the northernmost tip of Key Largo that must be avoided. Alligators and especially crocodiles are unpredictable and, despite a sluggish appearance, are extremely dangerous to humans.

# Equipment

Snorkeling tours include use of a mask, snorkel and inflatable safety vest. Swim fins are almost always part of the deal and are an added benefit. They make swimming much easier and will help you keep pace with the parade of fish you'll be joining. If you plan on a lot of snorkeling, by all means purchase your own equipment. A proper-fitting mask and a comfortable snorkel make the experience much more rewarding.

Masks and snorkels are made from rubber or silicone. The silicone is more expensive, but softer against the skin and somewhat more comfortable for prolonged use. Don't mix. Oils in rubber will badly discolor silicone.

If you wear eyeglasses you may want to invest in an optically corrected mask before your trip. They start at about $95 and can be ordered from most dive shops. You can wear contacts with a standard mask, but run the risk of losing them underwater. Expect difficulty sealing your mask if you sport a beard or mustache. Water tends to wick in along the hairs. Try a bit of vaseline around the rim of your mask. It may reduce or eliminate the problem. Shaving is the most reliable solution.

Long hair should be brushed back, away from your face, before putting on a mask. One thin hair becomes a very efficient siphon of water. Check for a good fit by placing the mask against your face (without the straps) and inhale. If you can't easily shake the mask off, the fit is good.

*Sea turtle.*

NEVER USE EAR PLUGS OR SWIMMING GOGGLES FOR SNORKELING. Pressure from even a very shallow dive can cause mask squeeze. Your nose must be included in the mask to allow you to exhale slightly and equalize the pressure as you descend. Use of ear plugs underwater can cause serious and permanent damage to your eardrums.

Before boarding the snorkel tour boat, be sure to pick up a container of anti-fogging solution. Available in most dive shops, it will keep the glass part of your mask crystal clear. Without it your mask will quickly fog up. In a pinch, if anti-fog solution is unavailable, rub a bit of saliva around the inside of the glass and rinse lightly.

During winter the water temperature drops from 85° down to 70-75°F. Some wetwear is desirable. A shorty wetsuit or a lycra wetskin will protect you from the sun and keep you warm. Wetskins are the most popular with snorkelers as they are easier to put on than wetsuits and cost a lot less. They will protect you from sunburn too – often the biggest problem a snorkeler encounters. While snorkeling, a thin layer of water over your back keeps you feeling deceptively cool, but does nothing to block out the harmful rays of the sun. Be safe.

If you don't have a wetskin or light wetsuit, wear a long-sleeved shirt and consider long pants if you are fair-skinned.

## Look, But Don't Touch

Everything living is protected in Florida's marine parks. Wearing gloves, touching corals and feeding fish are prohibited. Spearfishing is outlawed. Certain foods eaten by humans can be unhealthy and often fatal to fish. Touching corals may kill them or cause infection or disease which can spread to surrounding corals. Touching any corals may cause an allergic reaction, but touching fire coral will give you a painful sting.

It is best to familiarize yourself with the marine life before you visit the reefs. Fish and coral identification books and submersible sheets can be picked up at dive shops.

Avoid wearing dangling jewelry. To a normally harmless but somewhat toothy barracuda it may offer the same appeal as a fishing lure.

Display a diver-down flag any time you are in the water.

## Snorkeling Tours

Half-day tours to the underwater sanctuaries lead in popularity, but if you are after adventure you'll find numerous sail-snorkel trips that visit remote islands and shoals. New shallow-draft trimarans and catamarans designed for snorkeling visit out-islands and

*Fish feeding, Key West.*

 HEALTHY ALTERNATIVE FOR FISH FEEDING

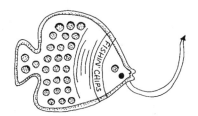

Fishin' Chips, a new all-natural fish food sold in dive shops, is gaining popularity with Keys snorkelers.

Each fish-shaped cardboard dispenser holds 28 waterproof pop-out pills and retails for about $4. Easy to tote, with a recyclable lanyard that slips over the wrist, the pills have been depth-tested to 130 feet. Air- and watertight packaging keeps the tablets dry until use. They don't cloud the water. ☎ 1-800-522-2469 for additional information. And be sure to recycle the packaging!

shallow reefs. Seaplane fly-in excursions to the Dry Tortugas, a magnificent chain of remote, uninhabited, coral-fringed islands, leave from Key West.

If you're traveling with scuba-equipped companions, you'll find most dive boats allow you to join the tour for a fee. Stop in at any dive shop for trip schedules. But the best trips are aboard the snorkel boats. They park on the shallow reefs and usually visit more than one site. Or you can spend a week aboard one of the live-aboard sailing yachts and tour the entire area.

Physical fitness buffs may wish to combine paddling with snorkeling tours. Both Key West Kayak and Mosquito Coast make that offer (see Canoe Tours chapter for listings).

Half-day snorkeling tours average $25, with some as high as $50. Camera and video rentals or use of special gear are extra.

## Biscayne National Park

Biscayne National Park is the largest marine park in the United States, consisting of 181,500 acres of islands, bays and offshore coral reefs. Snorkeling excursions are offered by **Biscayne National Underwater Park, Inc.**, P.O. Box 1270, Homestead FL 33030, ☎ 305-230-1100.

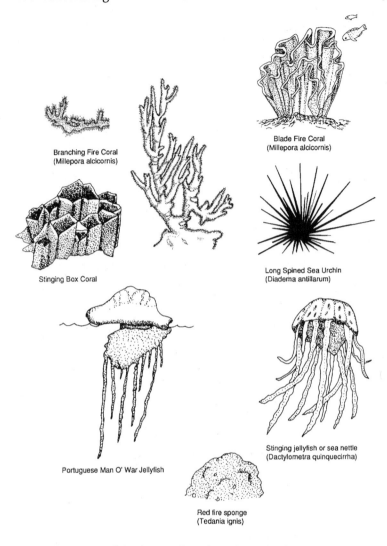

Branching Fire Coral
(Millepora alcicornis)

Blade Fire Coral
(Millepora alcicornis)

Stinging Box Coral

Long Spined Sea Urchin
(Diadema antillarum)

Portuguese Man O' War Jellyfish

Stinging jellyfish or sea nettle
(Dactylometra quinquecirrha)

Red fire sponge
(Tedania ignis)

*Stinging corals and marine animals.*

# Key Largo

Southeast of the Florida Peninsula, where the Keys stretch across the Gulf of Mexico and Atlantic, lies one of nature's oldest and most artfully crafted underwater gardens, the **Key Largo National Marine Sanctuary**. Located in the Atlantic Ocean, the park sits three miles off Key Largo and extends eight miles out to the edge of the continental shelf. Designated a National Marine Sanctuary it encompasses 100 square miles of submerged coral reefs. More than one million divers and snorkelers visit the sanctuary each year.

Snorkeling trips to the park are offered by the following tour operators: **Coral Reef Park Co.**, MM 102.5 (inside John Pennekamp State Park, ☎ 305-451-1621), the **Sun Diver Station Snorkel Shacks**, MM 103, Bayside (☎ 451-2220) or at the Best Western docks, MM 100, Oceanside (☎ 451-9686), **Silent World Dive Center**, MM 103.2 (☎ 451-3252), **Upper Keys Dive and Sport Center** (☎ 853-0526), **It's a Dive** (☎ 453-9881), **Scuba-Do Charters**, MM 100 (☎ 451-3446), **Sharky's Inc**, MM 106 Plaza (☎ 451-5533), **Divers City**, MM 104, Oceanside (☎ 451-4554), **Ocean Divers**, MM 100 (☎ 451-1113), **The Keys Diver**, MM 100 (☎ 451-1177), and aboard the *HMS Minnow*, MM 100, Holiday Inn docks (☎ 451-7834), **American Diving Headquarters, Inc.** is at MM 105.5 (☎ 305-451-0037). Snorkel tours usually leave the park docks at 9 am, noon and 3 pm.

**Captain Corky's Divers' World** at MM 99.5 offers custom snorkeling charters, including three-and five-day live-aboard trips. ☎ 451-3200. Write to P.O. Box 1663, Key Largo FL 33037.

# Islamorada

Offshore from Islamorada, on the Atlantic side, lie the remains of the 287-ton Dutch ship, *San Pedro*, one of Florida's oldest artificial reefs. The ship rest in a sand pocket 18 feet below the surface, offering shelter to a host of sea creatures amidst the ballast stones and coral overgrowth. Visibility can't compare with the offshore reefs, but it is an interesting dive nonetheless. Residents include gobies, damsels, moray eels and groupers.

The ship carried 16,000 pesos in Mexican silver and numerous crates of Chinese porcelain when she wrecked in 1733. For tours, contact the **Long Key State Park** office at ☎ 664-4815. Boaters use LORAN coordinates 14082.1, 43320.6. The wreck lies approximately 1¼ nautical miles south from Indian Key. Be sure to tie up to the mooring buoys to prevent anchor damage.

Islamorada dive shops visit **Molasses**, **Alligator** and **Tennessee reefs** – all named for a ship wrecked at the site and in depths ranging from extremely shallow to about 40 feet.

Sign up for an Islamorada snorkeling trip at the **Holiday Isle Dive Center**, MM 84.9 (☎ 664-4145).

Daily reef and wreck tours are also offered at **Bud n' Mary's Dive Center**, MM 79.8, (☎ 664-2211) and **World Down Under**, MM 81.5, (☎ 664-9312).

## Marathon - Big Pine Key

**Sombrero Reef** and **Looe Key National Marine Sanctuary** both offer superb reef snorkeling. Depths range from two to 35 feet.

**Marathon Divers**, MM 54 (☎ 289-1141), offers daily reef trips.

In Big Pine Key book a tour with **Underseas Inc.** at MM 30.5, (☎ 872-2700).

Excursions to the island where *PT 109* was filmed can be arranged through **Strike Zone Charters** (☎ 800-654-9560 or 305-872-9863). On the 4½-hour trip, owners Mary & Larry Threlkeld include snorkeling gear and a fish fry on the beach. Write to Strike Zone Charters, Dolphin Marina, MM 28.5, Rt. 1, Box 610 D, Big Pine Key FL 33043.

# Key West

Key West offers perhaps the most diversified collection of adventure-snorkeling cruises in the islands. Sail-snorkel cruises visit secluded islands surrounded with beautiful coral reefs, often including lunch and refreshments.

Captain Ron Canning cruises with several local pods of dolphins and offers dolphin-watch snorkeling excursions aboard the luxury catamaran, *Patty C* (☎ 294-6306). Prior reservations a must.

On neighboring Stock Island, personalized charters can be arranged aboard the six-passenger trimaran, *Fanta Sea* (☎ 305-296-0362).

History buffs will want to book a snorkel trip on Key West's largest tall ship, the 86-ft wooden windjammer *Appledore* (☎ 296-9992). Half-day reef trips depart at 10:30 am and 3:30 pm.

The 65-ft schooner, *Reef Chief* (☎ 292-1345) offers custom snorkeling charters.

Sail-racing fans will delight in touring the out-islands aboard the *Stars & Stripes*, a huge 54-ft, 49-passenger replica of the racing catamaran made famous by Dennis Conner. This ninth version was designed especially for cruising the shallow channels and reefs of Key West. For maximum comfort and enjoyment, this sailing yacht features a 29-ft beam, glass-bottom viewing, and a fully shaded lounge. The ultra shallow draft (25 inches) allows the captain to pull up to sandy beaches at Woman Key and other spots that are off-limits to many charter boats. See the *Stars & Stripes* at Land's End Marina (☎ 294-7877 or 800-634-MEOW). You can book a tour at Lost Reef Adventures, 261 Margaret Street, Key West.

Three more fabulous catamarans, the 60-ft *Fury*, *Queen Conch* and *Reef Express* offer sail-snorkel tours out of Key West. The *Fury* (☎ 294-8899) departs from the Truman Annex (west end of Greene St.) at 9:30 am and 1:00 pm; it visits Sand Key, Rock Key, Eastern Dry Rocks and Western Sambo – all coral reef out-islands. The *Queen Conch* (☎ 295-9030) departs Conch Harbor Marina off N. Roosevelt Avenue, and includes equipment, soft drinks, lunch and snorkel gear.

The *Reef Express* offers three-hour trips departing from the end of William St. Trip includes sanitized snorkel gear, instruction, flotation devices and cold soft drinks.

*Sunny Days*, a large sailing catamaran, departs the dock at the end of William St. Trips of 3½ hours depart at 9 am and 1 pm. Includes gear, instruction and cold sodas. Beer and wine after snorkeling.

**Reef Raiders Dive Inc.** offers snorkeling trips aboard the 53-ft catamaran *El Gato*, departing 9:30 and 1:30. Beer, wine and soda included on all tours.

**Witt's End Charters** (☎ 305-304-0139) at Land's End Marina offers personalized weekend to 10-day charters aboard the beautiful 51-ft sailing yacht, *Witt's End*. Includes meals, captain and chef (who also happens to be a Coast Guard-certified captain), snorkel gear, dive compressor, and fishing equipment. Expert snorkeling instruction. Optional wedding packages. Reservations a must. Write to Captains Witt, P.O. Box 625, Key Largo FL 33037.

# Dry Tortugas

The Dry Tortugas, an uninhabited island group lying 70 miles off Key West, sit in the midst of a pristine shallow reef tract, ideal for snorkeling, with vibrant staghorn thickets, hordes of fish and abundant critters. On calm days, both high-speed ferry and seaplane tours depart for Garden Key, site of the Fort Jefferson Monument. Seaplane tours are half-day; the ferry departs Key West at 8 am and returns at 7 pm. Bring a picnic lunch, cold drinks and snorkeling equipment.

Spanish explorer Ponce de Leon discovered these island in 1513 and named them Las Tortugas, meaning the Turtles, for the throngs of turtles around the islands. The modern name, Dry Tortugas, came about as a way to warn sea travelers that the islands have no fresh water. In any case, the great numbers of loggerhead turtles are gone, but not all. Most snorkelers spot at least one or two. The trips are expensive, at this writing $130 for the seaplane trip and $75 for the ferry.

The Marquesas, equally magnificent in reef life, are approachable only in periods of exceptionally calm seas by private boat. Navigation information is available though the US Coast Guard.

On the 30-mile crossing to the Marquesas you can spot sharks and rays as they dart under the boat along the sandy bottom. Armies of tulip shells with resident hermit crabs guard the remote island beaches.

Seaplane-snorkel tours to the Dry Tortugas can be booked with **Key West Seaplane**, Junior College Rd. ☎ 305-294-6978.

The *Yankee Freedom*, a 100-ft high-speed ferry, features an air-conditioned cabin, spacious sundeck, complete galley, complimentary breakfast and full bar. ☎ 305-294-7009 or 800-634-0939.

## Tips For Boaters

Be sure to display a diver's flag if you are snorkeling from your own boat. Strong currents may be encountered on the outside reefs. Check before disembarking. One person should always remain on board.

Be aware of weather, sea conditions and your own limitations before going offshore. Sudden storms, waterspouts and weather-related, fast-moving fronts are not uncommon. Nautical charts are available at marinas and boating supply outlets throughout the Keys.

Key Largo and Looe Key National Marine Sanctuaries provide mooring buoys to which you should attach your boat rather than anchor. If no bouys are available, you should drop anchor only in sand. The bottom in sandy areas appears white.

In protected parts of the Keys, destruction of coral formations through grounding or imprudent anchoring can lead to penalties and fines of up to $50,000. Fines for minor damage to coral start at $150. Give yourself plenty of room to maneuver.

For Key Largo National Marine Sanctuary, use chart 11451 or 11462, and for Looe Key National Marine Sanctuary use chart 11442 or 11445.

# Swim With The Dolphins

If you are fascinated by dolphins, a unique and unusual encounter awaits you in any one of three Florida Keys facilities – a chance to interact freely with the gentle animals. Instead of simply sitting back amused with watching the beautiful creatures perform, you can now splash in their pool and join in their playful stunts.

You must be at least 13 years old, know how to swim and attend an orientation session with a dolphin trainer. Life jackets available. Advance reservations are a must.

The in-water sessions are 30 minutes. A trainer is in charge at all times, yet once you are comfortable in the water you are encouraged to be creative and very active, to interact by diving down with mask and snorkel.

When you first enter the water the dolphins will "turn on" their sonar and check you over. You will hear a clicking, whistling sound. Once their get-acquainted ritual is complete, they may present a chin to be scratched or kissed. When they roll to one side showing their dorsal fins, it's a way of telling guests to grab hold and take an exciting ride through the water.

Don't be alarmed if one comes charging straight at you with lightning speed. They like to play "chicken" and will veer off to one side at the last moment. Of course, no one can ever predict entirely how an animal taken from the wild will behave, but these individuals are carefully screened for gentle character and the right personality.

# Where To Do It

Located on Grassy Key near Marathon, the **Dolphin Research Center** maintains liaisons with university research programs and independent investigators around the world. A not-for-profit teaching and research facility, the center has received national attention when called upon to accept sick or wounded dolphins found in coastal waters.

"Our dolphins really enjoy contact with people, "says Mandy Rodriguez, director of the Dolphin Research Center. "Actually, they (the dolphins) think we are providing people for their fun and enjoyment."

The center also accepts dolphins from other marine research facilities at which the animals sometimes suffer from overcrowded conditions. Still more dolphins, "burnt out" from years of performing in aquariums, spend their "retirement" at the center and achieve a complete rejuvenation living in the warm waters of the Atlantic instead of in a tank.

Examination of these dolphins reveals remarkable similarities to humans beset by stressful circumstances, from simple loss of appetite to a full-blown case of bleeding ulcers. But with human attention and kindness, the animals return to good health and good spirits.

Islamorada-based **Theater of the Sea** offers swim programs three times a day, along with continuous marine shows featuring sea lions, sharks and other marine species. As part of the dolphin program, trainer Gina Gouvan has developed special exercises for spinal-cord-injured human patients. Interaction with the dolphins has been useful in easing depression and in community re-integration. The patients must be alert.

At **Dolphins Plus** on Key Largo, visitors enjoy much more than a dolphin swim. A special orientation program offers an hour-long pre-swim seminar about the endangered marine species.

There are additional field trips and dolphin-research programs offered. For more information, contact the dolphin facilities. Cost for the swim programs starts at $60.

**Dolphins Plus Inc.**, 147 Corrine Place, Key Largo 33037; ☎ 305-451-1993.

**Theatre of the Sea**, (MM 84), Islamorada FL 33036; ☎ 305-664-2431.

**Dolphin Research Center**, (MM 59), Grassy Key, Marathon FL
33050; ☎ 305-289-1121.
A new twist on swim-with-the-dolphins programs is offered by
Key West's Captain Ron Canning, who cruises offshore with several local pods of dolphins and offers snorkeling-with-wild-dol-
phins excursions aboard the luxury catamaran, *Patty C*
(☎ 305-294-6306). Prior reservations a must.

# Section III

*Hemingway House, Key West*

# Attractions

## Florida Keys

### KEY LARGO

**The African Queen,** made famous by Humphrey Bogart and Katharine Hepburn, sits at the Holiday Inn docks, MM 100. Sign up at the Holiday Inn gift shop for a half-hour ride aboard the *Queen.* ☎ 305-451-4655.

**Caribbean Shipwreck Museum & Research Institute,** MM 102.6, displays sunken treasure and rare maritime artifacts from around the world. ☎ 305-451-4655.

**Dolphins Plus,** MM 99.5, offers dolphin swims. See "Swim with the Dolphins" chapter. ☎ 305-451-1993.

**Key Largo Undersea Park** offers divers a tour or stay at the world's only underwater hotel, the Jules Undersea Lodge. Snorkeling tours also available. ☎ 451-2353.

**John Pennekamp Coral Reef State Park**, MM 102.5, features an aquarium, nature trails, marina, public boat ramp, gift shop, dive shop, camping, swimming, soft sand beach, snorkeling, scuba and glass-bottom boat tours. ☎ 305-451-1621.

## ISLAMORADA

**Theater of the Sea**, MM 84.5, Islamorada, occupies the old Flagler railroad excavations. Established in 1946, the resulting huge lagoon and marine park offers visitors a chance to shake hands or be kissed by a sea lion, touch a shark or stroke a turtle, feed a stingray or pet a dolphin. Continuous shows run from 9:30 am to 4 pm. The park, 74 miles south of Miami, offers continuous shows from 9:30 am to 4 pm. ☎ 305-664-2431. Write to P.O. Box 407, Islamorada FL 33036.

**Indian Key Historical Site**, MM 78.5. See "Boat Tours" chapter for details. ☎ 305-664-4815.

**Lignumvitae Botanical Site**, MM 78.5. Guided botanical tours by boat. ☎ 305-664-4815

**San Pedro Underwater State Park**, off Indian Key. The site of a 1733 shipwreck. Cannon replicas, trails, coral formations and schools of tropical fish make an interesting snorkeling spot.

**Treasure Village**, MM 86. **Historic Shipwreck Museum** offers a look at nautical artifacts. ☎ 305-852-0511.

## MARATHON

**Crane Point Hammock**, MM 50. This 64-acre densely wooded botanical preserve contains archaeological digs and natural treasures. ☎ 305-743-9100.

**Dolphin Research Center**, MM 50, offers impressive dolphin and sea lion performances, dolphin swims and educational walking tours. ☎ 305-289-1121.

**Key Colony Beach Golf Course**, MM 53.5. No tee times, clubs and pull carts, reasonable fees. ☎ 305-289-1533.

**Museum of Natural History and Children's Museum**, MM 50. Marine touch tanks, tropical fish feeding and nature trail. ☎ 305-743-9100.

The **Old Seven Mile Bridge** begins at MM 47. This bridge connects Marathon to the Lower Keys and is home to the Seven Mile Bridge Run and the world's longest fishing pier. A favorite cycling and hiking spot too.

**Pigeon Key**, a four-acre island located 2.2 miles west of Marathon. Served as a construction and maintenance camp for the old Flagler railroad. Today it is operated by a non-profit local organization dedicated to preserving the history and environment of the Keys through education and research. ☎ 305-289-0025.

## LOWER KEYS

**Bahia Honda State Park**, MM 37, features one of the top 10 beaches in North America. Marina, dive shop, cabins and camp sites. ☎ 305-872-2353.

**Bat Tower**, MM 17 on Sugarloaf Key. Remains of an early unsuccessful attempt to destroy mosquitoes by attracting bats to the area. ☎ 305-872-2411.

**Blue Hole & Jack Watson Nature Trail**, MM 30.5 in Big Pine Key. Blue Hole is a freshwater sinkhole inhabited by alligators and turtles. Observation area and small walking trail. One hundred yards ahead lies the Jack Watson Walking Trail, a two-thirds mile path with information on the flora and fauna of the Lower Keys. ☎ 305-872-2411.

**Coupon Bight State Aquatics Preserve**, MM 28.5 in Big Pine Key, separates the mainland from an oceanside peninsula. ☎ 305-872-2411.

**Great White Heron National Wildlife Refuge**, MM 28.5-31.5 in Big Pine Key. Home to many migratory birds in winter. Offers protection to rare and endangered species. ☎ 305-872-2239

## KEY WEST

**Audubon House and Gardens** display 18th- and 19th-century Audubon engravings and a gallery of porcelain bird sculptures. Formally the home of Captain John H. Geiger, the house has been restored as a museum to commemorate John James Audubon's 1832 visit to Key West. At 205 Whitehead Street, Key West FL 33040. ☎ 305-294-2116.

**Bahama Village** in the heart of Old Town features restaurants, bars, shops, public pool and playground. Home of the Goombay Festival.

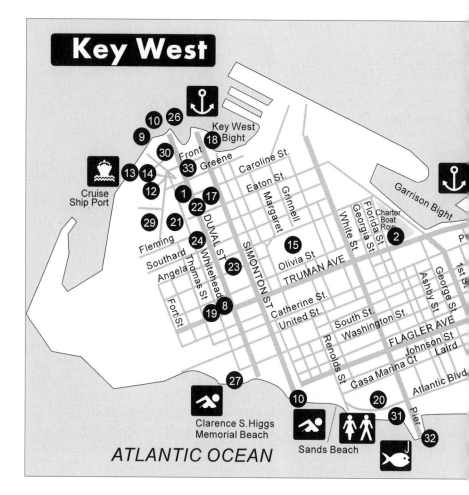

# Key West Attractions and Points of Interest

1. Audubon House
2. Charter Fishing Boats
3. & 33. Conch Train Depots
4. De Poo Hospital
5. East Martello Museum and Gallery
6. Florida Keys Memorial Hospital
7. Golf Course
8. Hemingway House
9. Hospitality House
10. Key West Beaches
11. Key Plaza Shopping Center
12. Mel Fisher's Treasure Museum
13. Key West Aquarium
14. Key West Chamber of Commerce
15. Key West City Cemetary
16. Key West International Airport

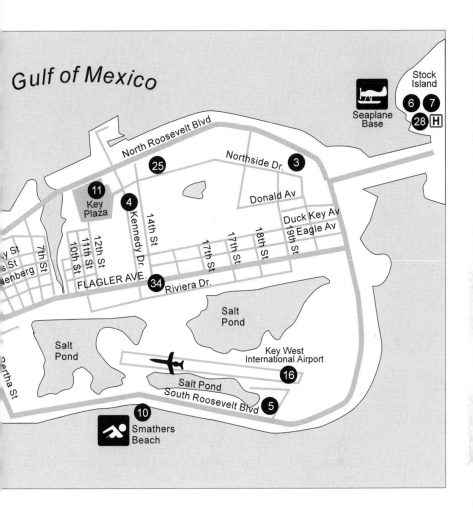

Gulf of Mexico

Stock Island

Seaplane Base

6  7
28  H

North Roosevelt Blvd

Northside Dr.   3

25

Donald Av

Duck Key Av
Eagle Av

11
Key Plaza

4

12th St
11th St
10th St

14th St

Kennedy Dr.

17th St

18th St
19th St

y St
s St
enberg

7th St

FLAGLER AVE.

34   Riviera Dr.

Salt Pond

Salt Pond

ertha St

Key West International Airport

16

Salt Pond
South Roosevelt Blvd

5

10
Smathers Beach

17. Key West Women's Club
18. Land's End Village
19. Lighthouse and Millitary Museum
20. Playground
21. & 34. Post Offices
22. Oldest House
23. Peggy Mills Garden
24. San Carlos Opera House

25. Searstown Shopping Center
26. Sightseeing Boat
27. Southernmost Point U.S.A.
28. Tennessee Williams Fine Arts Center
29. Truman's Little Whitehouse
30. Waterfront Playhouse
31. West Martello Tower
32. White Street Fishing Pier

*Conch Tour Train.*

**The Conch Tour Train** takes you on a 90-minute narrated tour of Key West. It is the fastest way to familiarize yourself with the entire city. Board the train at 601 Duval Street, Key West FL 33040. ☎ 305-294-5161.

**Old Town Trolley Tours** make 12 stops for sightseeing and shopping in Key West. Passengers may disembark for lunch and rejoin the tour later. Tours begin every 30 minutes. The station is at 1910 North Roosevelt Blvd., Key West FL 33040. ☎ 305-296-6688.

**Curry Mansion**, 511 Caroline Street in Old Town, displays 22 rooms of antiques, verandas and a widow's walk. ☎ 305-294-5349.

**Customs House** (under restoration), Front Street in Old Town. Considered Florida's finest example of Romanesque Revival architectiure, it originally housed the Post Office, US Customs Service, US District Court, the Internal Revenue Service and the Lighthouse Service. ☎ 305-296-3913.

**Donkey Milk House Museum.** Winner of a 1992 Restoration Award, this 1886 Greek Revival home is open to the public as a house museum full of unusual furnishings and rare features. Self-guided tour. Antique shop in front parlor. Open daily 10 am-5 pm. ☎ 305-296-1866.

**East Martello Museum and Art Gallery**, 3501 S. Roosevelt Blvd., adjacent to the Key West International Airport. This Civil War fort turned museum displays military artifacts from the Keys. Open daily, 9:30 am-5 pm. ☎ 305-296-3913.

**Ernest Hemingway House** was home to Ernest Hemingway and his second wife, Pauline, from 1931 to 1961. Now a registered National Historic Landmark, the house and gardens are where Hemingway wrote *For Whom the Bell Tolls, Green Hills of Africa, A Farewell to Arms, The Fifth Column* and *Snows of Kilimanjaro*. Descendents of Hemingway's cats roam the tropical grounds. Located at 907 Whitehead Street. ☎ 305-294-1575.

**Fort Jefferson National Monument** lies 68 miles west of Key West and may be reached by boat or seaplane. Self-guided tours of the fort are combined with snorkeling, sightseeing, camping, and bird-watching. For boating information, call the Coast Guard Base at ☎ 305-247-6211. For flights, contact Key West Seaplane Service, 5603 Junior College Road, Stock Island FL 33040, ☎ 305-294-6978 or 800-224-2359. For high-speed ferry service, contact Tortugas Ferry, ☎ 305-294-7009 or 800-634-0939. Park, ☎ 305-242-6713.

**Fort Zachary Taylor State Park and Beach** opens 8 am to sunset. A stronghold during the Civil War, the fort displays the largest collection of Civil War cannons in the US. It's off Duval St. Picnic grills. Spectacular sunsets. ☎ 305-292-6713.

**Jessie Porter's Heritage House Museum** offers a look at remnants of a rich and turbulent past. Antiques, treasures and odd shipwreck mementos collected by six generations of the Porter family. After the guided tour, relax in the garden to recordings of poety by family friend, Robert Frost. ☎ 305-296-3573.

**Mel Fisher's Maritime Heritage Society Museum** sits opposite the Audubon House. Fascinating gold and silver jewelry and treasures from the *Atocha* are displayed. You can touch a gold bar. Gems and coins from the wreck have been fashioned into jewelry and may be purchased. Reproductions of the coins are sold too. Located at 200 Greene St., Key West FL 33040. ☎ 305-294-9936.

**Higgs Beach.** Children's playground, long pier, sailboat rentals, barbecue grills, picnic tables and restrooms.

**The Key West Lighthouse Museum** is Florida's third oldest brick lighthouse. Climb 88 steps and view the entire city from the 90-ft observation level. Great photo opportunities. Located across the street from the Hemingway House in Old Town at 938 Whitehead Street, Key West FL 33040. ☎ 305-294-0012.

*Key West Lighthouse.*

**The Key West Aquarium**, opened in 1932, was the first tourism attraction built in the Florida Keys. The exhibit includes a living reef, displays of sharks, barracudas, angel fish and a turtle pool. There is a touch tank. A huge plastic shark outside makes a patient photo subject. The aquarium is on the waterfront at Mallory. The entrance is behind the shops. ☎ 305-296-2051. Write to One Whitehead Street, Key West FL 33040.

**The Key West Cemetery**, like the native inhabitants of this tiny, subtropical island, is unique. Filled with humor and history, one stone reads "I Told You I Was Sick." Carved into another headstone at a nearby grave is the self-consoling, tongue-in-cheek message of a grieving widow, "At Least I Know Where He's Sleeping Tonight." At a special memorial in the cemetery rest the bodies of those who died when the US Battleship *Maine* was sunk in Havana's Harbor in 1898, touching off the Spanish-American War. The cemetery fills 21 prime acres in the heart of the historic district. Tours available. ☎ 305-292-6718.

The **Key West Shipwreck Historeum** at 1 Whitehead Steet on Mallory Square combines interactive theater with a tour of the historic Asa Tift warehouse. Fascinating, the Historeum tour combines actors, films, laser technology and the actual artifacts from the recently rediscovered vessel *Isaac Allerton,* which sank in 1856.

**Ripley's Believe It Or Not Odditorium**, 527 Duval Street, covers 10,000 air-conditioned square feet in the old Strand Theater. Fifteen hundred exhibits offer interactive displays and a look at the bizarre and unusual. Worth a stop! ☎ 305-293-9896.

**Smather's Beach** at the end of Duval Street and S. Roosevelt Blvd offers parasailing, jet-ski rental and picnic tables.

*Tightrope walker, Mallory Square sunset celebration, Key West.*

**Tennessee Williams Fine Arts Center** on Stock Island, 5901 West College Road, features year-round opera, dance, symphonic and chamber music. National touring companies perform Shakespeare and current Broadway hits. ☎ 305-296-1520.

Situated in a former sea captain's home, the **Wrecker's Museum,** 322 Duval Street, exhibits old documents, ship models, undersea and maritime artifacts. Opens 10 am to 4 pm daily. ☎ 305-294-9502.

**Writers Walk** through Old Town Key West weaves a one-hour walk with a literary history of the island. ☎ 305-293-9291.

**Sunset Celebration.** If there is a single attraction that's a must for a Key West visit, it is the sunset at Mallory Square Pier. The place comes alive with entertainment. There is a unicyclist wriggling free of a straight jacket, two men tumbling while a woman plays a tune on a washboard and cymbals. A juggler delights the crowd first with oranges, then with flaming Indian clubs. Another juggler, after beating out rhythms on a bongo drum, dazzles the crowd with a tossed machete and flaming stick.

If you're hungry, the Cookie Lady seems to sense it, arriving on her bicycle, from which she hawks warm brownies and cookies.

The entertainment is free, but the entertainers do pass the hat. The standard pitch of two jugglers is: "We welcome your dollars. We welcome your complaints. If you have any complaints, write them on a five-dollar bill and put the bill in the plate." There are no complaints, but plenty of applause, loudest when the Key West sun drops into the sea.

## EVERGLADES

### Everglades City

**Eden of the Everglades**, on Route 29, two miles south of Hwy 41, offers boat tours, a unique wetlands zoo and scenic boat tours through wildlife habitats. Boats depart hourly starting at 11 am. Turn right before Everglades City Bridge. ☎ 1-800-543-3367.

**Jungle Erv's Everglades Information Station** on Route 29 in Everglades City features an alligator zoo, exotic birds and a petting zoo. ☎ 941-695-2805.

### Tamiami Trail

**Wooten's Air Boat Tours and Swamp Buggy Rides**, on US 41, two miles west of Ochopee, displays hundreds of alligators and live snakes. Everglades wilderness tours by airboat or swamp buggy depart every half-hour. ☎ 941-695-2781.

**The Miccosukee Indian Village**, MM 70, 25 miles west of Miami on the Tamiami Trail (US 41), is open daily, year round. Miccosukee craftsmen demonstrate woodcraft, doll making, basket weaving and intricate patchwork sewing. Lively alligator wres-

*Alligator wrestling.*

tling and airboat rides highlight the village activities. A museum features tribal films and artifacts. ☎ 305-223-8388 or 305-223-8380. Write to P.O. Box 440021, Miami FL 33144.

## Miami Area

**The Monkey Jungle**, off US 1 in South Dade, shelters nearly 500 primates, most running free on a 20-acre reserve. It is one of the few protected habitats for endangered primates in the United States and the only one that the general public can explore. You are caged and the monkeys run wild. To get to the park, take the Florida Turnpike's Homestead Extension (Hwy 821) south to the Cutler Ridge Blvd./SW 216 St. exit, get onto 216 St. westbound, then go west for five miles. Or take US 1 south to SW 216 St., then go west on 216 for 3½ miles. ☎ 305-235-1611. Write 14805 S.W. 216 St., Miami FL 33170.

**Miami Metrozoo** is open every day from 10 am to 5:30 pm. There are more than 2,800 magnificent wild animals living in a cageless, natural environment; Paws, a new children's petting zoo; the Zoofari Monorail, which takes you on an air-conditioned safari; elephant rides, koalas, flamingos, white tigers and a 1½-acre tropical aviary. Ticket booth closes at 4 pm. Metrozoo is about 20 minutes from Miami International Airport. From US 1, take SW 152nd Street exit west three miles to the entrance. From the Turnpike extension, take the SW 152nd Street exit west a quarter-mile to the Metrozoo entrance. ☎ 305-251-0403.

**Miami Seaquarium** is South Florida's largest marine attraction. Seals, sharks, dolphins and killer whales are the stars. Continuous shows. Magnificent aquariums. ☎ 305-361-5705. Located at 4400 Rickenbacker Causeway, Miami FL.

**Parrot Jungle and Gardens**, south of Miami International Airport off US 1, offers encounters with talking birds, walks through beautiful tropical gardens, trained-bird shows in the "Parrot Bowl" where macaws and cockatoos perform feats that defy the imagination. Besides the 1,100 parrots, there are huge alligators, giant tortoises, peacocks, exotic plants and a petting zoo. Fun for all ages. Open from 9:30 am to 6 pm. Admission: adults $9.75; chil-  dren $4. Wheelchairs and strollers available. ☎ 305-666-7834. Located at 11000 S.W. 57 Avenue, Miami FL 33156.

# Dining

Seafood, always abundant in the waters of the Gulf of Mexico and Florida Keys, has dictated many local food habits and preferences. Yellowtail, red snapper, shrimp, dolphin (the fish) and stone crab claws are prominent menu features. All come from local waters.

The alligator has been brought back from near extinction in part to make a nightly appearance as a house specialty – fried or broiled. But if your tastes don't run toward exotic, avoid dishes labeled "mixed seafood grill."

Stone crab claws are quite delectable and, in some minds, ecologically sound, as just one claw is removed and the live crab is then thrown back into the sea. The claw grows back. Divers and snorkelers exploring the reefs spot these curious crabs brandishing one huge claw and one tiny one.

Bahama food such as fish stew served with grits or bollos (pronounced bow-yows), an adaptation of Southern hush puppies made with mashed, shelled black-eyed peas instead of ground corn meal, is featured in many restaurants. A local dessert favorite is Key lime pie, made with condensed milk and the juice and minced rind of piquant Key limes that flourish in the area.

As the population of the area has grown and as tourism has grown to attract more than six million visitors a year, exotic dining inroads have been made. There now are restaurants featuring Polynesian, Japanese, Thai, Chinese, German, French, Greek and Italian cuisine.

As in any seaside area, raw bars are prominent. You will find oysters, sushi and clams, but conch is king. Served grilled, ground in burgers, fried in batters as fritters and raw in conch salad, it's all part of the local scene, along with wonderful, chewy crisp squid rings done in batter and deep-fried in a Mediterranean manner.

Cuban-influenced dishes are gaining in popularity. Flavored meats such as lechon, a roast of pork pungently flavored with garlic and tart sour oranges, ropa vieja (old clothes), a left-over dish, vaca fritao, a hamburger-caper cum-raisin concoction in a savory sauce are favorites. All are usually served with black beans and boiled white or yellow rice, flavored with either saffron or *bihol*.

Try them all. You'll find the south Florida cuisine a delight.

## Florida Keys Restaurants

### KEY LARGO

Key Largo is fast-food heaven, with popular chain restaurants everywhere. For all-day diving or fishing excursions, there are grocery stores and even gas stations that offer packaged lunches and cold beverages to go. **Miami Subs**, MM 100, Bayside, has subs and packaged goods to go. ☎ 451-3111. **Tower of Pizza**, MM 100, Oceanside, delivers fabulous New York-style pizza, sit down service too. ☎ 451-1461. Or try **Dominos Pizza**, Key Largo. ☎ 451-4951.

**Ballyhoo's Seafood Grille** is set in a 1930's conch house at MM 97.8 on the median. Fresh seafood specialties highlight the menu. Open daily. ☎ 852-0822.

Or try the **Cracked Conch**, MM 105, Oceanside (☎ 305-451-0732) for conch fritters and fried alligator, 90 different beers and honey biscuits. Low to moderate. ☎ 451-0732.

**The Fish House**, Oceanside at MM 102.4, serves excellent fresh fish, steaks and chicken for lunch or dinner. It is always packed, with a long waiting list after 6 pm. Moderate prices. Casual. ☎ 451-4665. Closes for two weeks in September.

**Frank Keys Café** offers romantic seating and decent Italian and seafood cuisine. MM 100.2, ☎ 453-0310.

**Holiday Casino Cruises**, MM 100, depart the Holiday Inn docks. They feature casino gambling in international waters. Complimentary hors d'oeuvres. Open bar and sandwiches or burgers available. Sunday brunch with fine catered food. Overnight packages. Sign up in the Holiday Inn lobby. ☎ 451-0000.

The **Italian Fisherman** offers dining on a waterfront terrace. Open daily from 11 am-10 pm. ☎ 451-4471.

The **Marlin Restaurant**, MM 102.7, is the favorite après-dive, story-swapping eatery. Open daily. ☎ 451-9555.

The **Pilot House** specializes in fresh local seafood and beef. Dockside. Turn off US 1 southbound after passing the Waldorf Plaza and TIB Bank onto Ocean Bay Drive. Pilot House is to the right on Sea Gate Blvd. Lunch and dinner. ☎ 451-3142.

For a unique tropical atmosphere and superb gourmet cuisine try the **Quay Restaurant**, MM 102.5, Bayside (☎ 451-0943). Indoor or garden seating. Moderate to expensive. Adjacent is the **Quay Mesquite Grill**, which serves excellent fried or broiled fish sandwiches. The complex also features a freshwater pool, boat docks, beach-side bar and entertainment. Sunset cruises.

**Senor Frijoles**, MM 103.9, Bayside, offers sizzling fajitas, seafood nachos, Mexican pizza, Cancun chili fish, enchiladas and chicken specials. ☎ 451-1592

Romantic starlight seating and gourmet seafood are also found at **Snooks Bayside Club**, MM 99.9, ☎ 453-3799. Moderate to high. Garden patio or indoor dining. (Behind Largo Honda.)

**Sundowners** on the bay at MM 104 specializes in seafood, chicken, steaks and pasta. Daily 11am-10 pm. Bayfront. ☎ 451-4502.

**Sushi Nami**, MM 99.5 at Marina del Mar, specializes in authentic Japanese cuisine – sushi and shimi, tempura, teriyaki, yakitori (shish kabab) or yakisoba, a mix of spice egg noodles with either beef, pork, chcken or vegetables. Lunch and dinner. ☎ 453-9798.

**Rick & Debbie's Tugboat Restaurant**, Oceanside at Seagate Blvd and Ocean Drive off MM 100, is a locals' favorite. Specials are fried or broiled fish. Low to moderate. Opens 11 am weekdays, weekends at 7 am. ☎ 453-9010.

Early breakfasts are served at **Howard Johnsons**, MM 102.5, ☎ 451-2032, **Harriets**, MM 95.7, ☎ 852-8689, **Holiday Inn**, MM 100, **Gilberts**, MM 107.9, ☎ 451-1133, and **Ganim's Kountry Kitchen**, MM 102, ☎ 451-3337, and MM 99.6 across from Holiday Inn. Or turn off Hwy 1 southbound at MM 103.5. Head towards the ocean on Transylvania Ave to find **The Hideout**, a local favorite for breakfast and lunch.

## ISLAMORADA

Islamorada's grills sizzle with fresh seafood and the most unique dining experiences in the Keys. You'll find the hot spot for fast food on the shores of **Holiday Isle**, MM 84, Oceanside. Food stands line this sprawling beach complex with barbecued everything. Ice cream and pretzel vendors crowd in alongside the Keys' most dazzling display of string bikinis. Or take the elevator to the sixth-floor restaurant for a quieter view of the sea. Prices rise with the elevation.

**The Coral Grill**, MM 83.5, Bayside, features a nightly buffet. Great strawberry daiquiris! Sun. 12 pm-9 pm, weekdays 4:30-10 pm. ☎ 664-4803.

**The Green Turtle Inn**, MM 81.5, has an old time Keys' atmosphere and excellent cuisine. Wood-paneled walls are covered with celebrity photos. Leave room for their rum pie. Gets crowded after 6 pm. 5 pm-10 pm. Closed Mondays. ☎ 664-9031.

Enjoy sunset views and fresh seafood at **The Lorelei Restaurant,** MM 82, Bayside. Sun.-Thurs., 5-10 pm. The outdoor Cabana Bar features burgers, fish sandwiches, breakfasts, lunches, dinners and a raw bar. 7am-12pm. Entertainment on weekends. Drive or boat to it. ☎ 664-4656.

**Marker 88** offers exotic fish and steak entrées in a romantic setting. Choose from expertly prepared Scampi Mozambique, Snapper Rangoon, Lobster Marco Polo and a host of other gourmet creations. Closed Mondays. Reservations a must. MM 88, Plantation Key. Moderate to expensive. ☎ 305-852-9315.

**Cheeca Lodge** offers casual dining at the **Ocean Terrace Grill**, MM 81.5. Moderate to high. ☎ 664-4651.

**Plantation Yacht Harbor**, MM 87. Live bands. Lobster, stone crab, oysters and clams. Sunday brunch with omelette and waffle bar. Daily 11am-9 pm. ☎ 852-2381.

**Rip's Island Ribs 'N Chicken**, within the same complex, features do-it-your-way meals. Diners prepare their entrées on thick granite slabs that are heated to 600 degrees and brought to your table. Your waitress supplies hot garlic bread, fresh, ready-to-cook vegetables and a choice of sirloin, chicken or shrimp or a combination. Just toss a little salt on your rock and give your food a turn or two until it looks right. A choice of sauces adds the finishing touch. It's easy. Or. . . try the ribs. They're served cooked. Expect a long waiting line on weekends, especially in season. ☎ 664-5300.

**Squid Row**, MM 81.9, Oceanside, offers excellent fish dishes and excellent service. Open for lunch or dinner. ☎ 664-9865.

**Whale Harbor Restaurant** features an all-you-can-eat seafood buffet nightly. Huge selection. Lovely setting in the old Islamorada lighthouse, adjacent to the Islamorada docks at MM 83.5. Moderate. ☎ 664-4959.

Try a hand-tossed pizza or pasta at **Woody's**, MM 82. Family dining in the early evening. Late night food with adult entertainment every night but Monday. Inexpensive. ☎ 664-4335.

**Ziggy's: The Conch Restaurant**, MM 83.5, Bayside. A famous local landmark with 50s ambience features veal, lobster, native fish and local specials. Closed Wednesdays. ☎ 664-3391.

For a quick meal try a pita sandwich or a yogurt dish at the **Ice Cream Stoppe**, MM 80.5. ☎ 664-5026.

## LONG KEY

**Little Italy Restaurant** at MM 68.5 serves early breakfast, plus lunch and dinner. Italian specialties, fresh seafood and steaks in a cozy atmosphere. Open 6:30 am-2 pm, 5 pm-10 pm. Low to moderate. ☎ 664-4472.

## DUCK KEY

**Duck Key Emporium** offers subs and sandwiches, chili, pizza, black beans and rice, barbecued pork, salads. Dockside patio dining. 9 pm-6 pm, Mon.-Sat. ☎ 743-2299.

**Hawk's Cay Resort and Marina**, MM 61, features **The Cantina** for poolside lunch and dinners, **Porto Cayo** for elegant dining, Tue.-Sun. 6 pm to 10 pm, **The Palm Terrace** for buffet-style breakfast, 7 am to 10:30 am, and **WaterEdge** for dinner, 5:30 to 10 pm. Reservations, ☎ 743-7000.

## MARATHON

Marathon is a heavily populated residential community with a wide choice of restaurants. The best in atmosphere and fine dining is **Kelsey's** at MM 48.5. Moderate to high. ☎ 743-9018.

Fishing guides and boat captains swap tales at the **Anglers Lounge**, MM 48, above Kelsey's at Faro Blanco Resort. Open for lunch and dinner. Moderate. ☎ 743-9018.

**The Hurricane Raw Bar & Restaurant** at MM 49. 5 features more than 6,000 sq ft of raw bar, two cocktail bars, two dining rooms, and live entertainment. Specialties are hot and spicy chicken wings, fresh clams, oysters and conch. Lunch and dinner, 11 am-12 pm. Moderate. ☎ 743-5755.

**Key Colony Inn**, MM 54 at Key Colony Beach, features well-prepared seafood specialties. ☎ 743-0100.

**Latigo Charters**, MM 47.5, end of 11th St next to Shucker's. Features gourmet dinner cruises aboard a 56-ft motor yacht. Choose from three entrées. Complimentary wine, beer and champagne served with the meal. ☎ 289-1066.

Enjoy natural foods, vegetarian delights or grilled seafood on the porch of a charming 1935 stone house at **Mangrove Mama's**, MM 20. Open for lunch and dinner. Full take-out menu too. Moderate. Reservations, ☎ 745-3030.

Fast take-out food at low prices is featured at **Porky's Too** on the Marathon side of the Seven Mile Bridge. ☎ 289-2065.

Enjoy indoor or outdoor patio dining at the **Quay of Marathon**, MM 54. Lunch and dinner. ☎ 289-1810.

Early breakfasts are served at the **Holiday Inn**, MM 54, **Stuffed Pig**, MM 49, and **The Wooden Spoon**, MM 50.5, Sugarloaf Key.

## KEY WEST

You'll find the locals' favorite watering hole at **The Half Shell Raw Bar** in Lands End Village. Menu features are fried or broiled fish, shrimp and conch; raw oysters and clams. Friendly service. Try for a table on the back porch overlooking the docks, where you'll spot six or seven huge silver tarpon. Open for lunch and dinner. Moderate. ☎ 294-7496.

Across the wharf sits **Turtle Kraals Bar and Restaurant**, offering fresh fish, hamburgers and the largest selection of imported beers in Key West. The restaurant is what remains of the days when turtles were brought in by the boat load from as far away as the Cayman Islands and Nicaragua. ☎ 294-2640.

Kraals is an Afrikan word meaning holding pen or enclosure. It refers to the concrete pilings that were driven into the ocean bottom to form a holding pen for the turtles until they could be shipped to the Northeast or slaughtered and made into soup in the cannery.

**The Crab House**, 2001 S. Roosevelt Blvd. At the Sheraton suites. Serves stone crabs, shrimp, lobster, famous garlic and steamed crabs. Breakfast buffet 7-10:30 am, dinner 4-10 pm. ☎ 294-1370.

**The Crab Shack**, 908 Caroline St. across from Land's End Village, serves spicy steamed shrimp and crab dishes. Charcoal-grilled steaks and prime rib. A local's favorite. Daily 11 am to 10:30 pm. ☎ 294-9658.

**Louis' Back Yard** at the corner of Vernon & Waddell Streets is one of Key West's finest waterfront restaurants. American cuisine highlights the menu for lunch, dinner and Sunday brunch. Expensive. Louis' delightful patio bar sits over the sea. ☎ 294-1061.

**Mallory Market**, the center of the Historic Key West Waterfront, offers every imaginable fast-food eatery and a few you may not have thought of. One particularly good one is the conch fritter stand outside the Shipwreck Historeum, directly across from the Key West Aquarium.

**Pepe's Cafe**, 806 Caroline St., serves the best breakfasts in the Keys. Frosted glasses of fresh orange juice and artfully prepared French toast or egg dishes are served indoors or outside under a canopy of flowering vines. Pub-style fare for lunch and dinner. Outdoor decor includes a white picket fence with passerby peep holes at two levels – one for people and one for their pets. Charming. ☎ 294-7192.

## Duval Street

Duval Street's wonderful cafés and restaurants feature varied ethnic dishes.

**Bagatelle**, 115 Duval St., features indoor or outdoor gourmet dining in a magnificent Victorian mansion. Lunch and dinner daily. Moderate to expensive. ☎ 296-6609.

**The Banana Café**, 1211 Duval St. French restaurant and creperie. Open daily except Tues. for breakfast and lunch from 8 am to 3 pm. Dinner from 7 pm-10:30 pm. ☎ 294-7227.

**The Cheese Board** at 1075 Duval St. offers 52 varieties of cheese, coffees and wines. ☎ 294-0072.

**Chops** at the Holiday Inn, 430 Duval St., features venison chops, duck breast, rabbit, and seafood. 5:30-10:30 pm. ☎ 296-2991.

Exotic dishes from Southeast Asia are found at **Dim Sum**, 613 Duval St (rear). Dinner. ☎ 294-6230.

**Hog's Breath Saloon** packs guests into its bustling open-air restaurant and raw bar. Nightly entertainment from sunset to 2 am. "Hog's breath is better than no breath at all!" ☎ 296-4222.

**Kelly's Caribbean Bar, Grill & Brewery**, 301 Whitehead St., serves lunch, dinner or cocktails. Decent Caribbean cuisine in a tropical garden setting. Try one of their micro-brew beers. Original home of Pan American Airways, now owned by actress, Kelly McGillis. ☎ 293-8484.

The rooftop lounge at Holiday Inn's **La Concha**, 430 Duval Street, serves exotic island drinks and is the best spot in town for sunset viewing. Afterward, go downstairs to **Chops** for a sizzling steak dinner. ☎ 296-2991.

**Olive Oils Café** at 708 Duval Street features creative Mediterranean cuisine in a garden setting. Sunday brunch. Fixed-price menu. Lunch and dinner. ☎ 294-8994.

**Savannah**, 915 Duval St., serves up southern cooking in a lovely old conch house or garden. Daily from 6:30 pm. ☎ 296-6700.

**South Beach Seafood & Raw Bar** on the beach at the end of Duval St. – across from Southernmost House – offers the best in Key West atmosphere. Ribs, chicken, steak, oysters, clams. Full bar. Dine inside or out. Open 7 am to 10 pm. ☎ 294-2727.

**Yo Sake** at 722 Duval (☎ 294-2288) and **Kyushu** (☎ 294-2995) at 921 Truman Avenue feature Japanese cuisine and sushi bars. Lunch and dinner.

Strip malls along N. Roosevelt Blvd. feature most fast food chain restaurants: **Boston Market, Burger King, Wendy's, TGI Fridays, Shoney's, New York Pizza Café, Kenny Rogers, Howard Johnson, Carvel Ice Cream, Arby's Roast Beef.**

# Key West Nightlife

**Captain Hornblower's**, 300 Front St. Live jazz Thurs.-Sat., 9 pm-1 am. Sun. jazz jam 1-3 pm and 8 pm-1am. ☎ 294-4922.

Named for Ernest Hemingway's favorite 1930's bar (actually across the street) **Sloppy Joe's** is a Key West tradition. The huge building vibrates with live music and memorabilia. At the corner of Duval and Greene Sts.

**Captain Tony's Saloon**, 428 Green St., the original "Sloppy Joes" and a favorite Hemingway haunt. Live entertainment 8 pm to midnight. Sun. 3 pm-12 am. ☎ 294-1838.

**Dirty Harry's**, 208 Duval St. at the back of Alice's Alley, features live rock and roll. 8 pm to 2 am. ☎ 296-5513.

**Hog's Breath Saloon**, 400 Front St., features live entertainment daily, 1 pm-2 am. ☎ 296-4222.

**Margaritaville**, 500 Duval St. Bands from across the country perform rock and roll, rhythm and blues. Jimmy Buffett makes an occasional appearance. ☎ 292-1435.

**Nick's Bar and Grill** at the Hyatt Key West, on the Gulf at Simonton and Front Streets. Reggae and

jazz, sunset till 11 pm except Sunday. ☎ 296-9900.

**Pier House**, One Duval St. Live entertainment and dancing at Havana Docks. ☎ 296-4600.

**Turtle Kraals** at the Gulf end of Margaret St. in Lands End Village. Turtle races Tues., Thurs. and Sun. at 10 pm. Local guitarist and singer at 9 pm. ☎ 294-2640.

**Rumrunner Cruise**, 201 William St. Floating party, reggae and limbo dancing nightly. Sunset Cruise 6-7:30 pm, Sat. 9 pm-11:30. Watersports Island Party 12:45-5 pm. ☎ 293-1999.

## Everglades Restaurants

In Everglades City stop in at **The Captain's Table**, 102 Collier Blvd., ☎ 941-695-2727. Or **The Rod and Gun Club Resort**, ☎ 941-695-2101, once an exclusive hideaway for statesmen and movie stars. Cypress-wood paneling and trophy fish adorn the walls. Both restaurants offer seafood and steaks. Prices from $10.

**Oyster House Restaurant** on Highway 29 features a fresh oyster bar, local seafood and carry-out service. Open for lunch or dinner. ☎ 941-695-2073.

*Everglades Rod and Gun Club Restaurant.*

**The Miccosukee Indian Village Restaurant**, adjacent to Shark Valley on the Tamiami Trail, offers a variety of Indian dishes, from a Miccosukee burger to a typical American menu. ☎ 305-223-8388 or 223-8380.

## Flamingo Restaurant

**Flamingo Lodge** offers seafood and steaks at low to moderate prices. It is the only restaurant in Everglades National Park located at the end of the Main Park Road. The Flamingo camp store offers snack food, packaged sandwiches, coffee and sodas. Both are closed from May to November. ☎ 305-253-2241.

# Accommodations

Resort and motel rates vary with the time of year, the high season being mid-December to mid-April. Check with your travel agent or the resort for money-saving packages. Some are only three days, but save hundreds of dollars. Several tour operators offer four-day or longer stays that include airfare, meals and diving or fishing. Rates as indicated for each hotel are as follows (they drop considerably for stays longer than seven days):

| | |
|---|---|
| Low | $55 to $85 |
| Moderate | $95 to $105 |
| Deluxe | $110 and up |

Major credit cards are accepted at all of the resorts and large motels. Some of the smaller motels ask for cash only. All hotels listed have air conditioning and color TV.

## Florida Keys

Keys accommodations range from informal housekeeping cottages, simply-furnished bayside motels, spacious, condo and house rentals, to luxurious resort villages, houseboats, and campgrounds, most of which are packed tight with RV's. All accommodations are air-conditioned and most have cable-color TV and a refrigerator in the room.

*Amoray Lodge hotelier, Amy Slate, cozies up to the dive buddy for whom she named the resort.*

Some of the older mom-and-pop motels on the bay have been updated and restored, offering a certain island charm that is hard to duplicate in the large resorts. A few are badly in need of renovation and also are parking areas for RV's. Send for current brochures.

## KEY LARGO ACCOMMODATIONS

For a complete list of home rental agencies, contact the **Key Largo Chamber of Commerce**, 106000 Overseas Hwy., Key Largo FL 33037. ☎ 305-451-1414, US 800-822-1088, fax 305-451-4726, e-mail www.floridakeys.org.

**Amy Slate's Amoray Lodge** on Florida Bay offers 16 ultra-clean, attractive, modern one- and two-bedroom apartments with full kitchens. Air-conditioned and ceiling fans. Sundeck. Scuba, snorkel and boat trips leave for Pennekamp Park from the resort dock aboard luxurious catamaran, *Amoray Dive*. Walking distance to several good restaurants. A great choice for Pennekamp divers. Low to deluxe. No pets. ☎ 800-426-6729 or 305-451-3595. Fax, 305-453-9516.

**Anchorage Resort & Yacht Club**, MM107.5, bayside, sits on the northern tip of Key Largo, away from the mainstream of activity. The resort features a fishing pier, laundry, tennis court, deck, balconies, and grills. Boat docking. Deluxe. Write 107800 Overseas Hwy, Key Largo FL 33037. No pets. ☎ 305-451-0500, fax 305-232-1516.

**Baycove Motel**, MM 99.5, bayside, offers 11 clean, newly remodeled rooms. Boat dock. Pets OK. Low to deluxe. ☎ 305-451-1686.

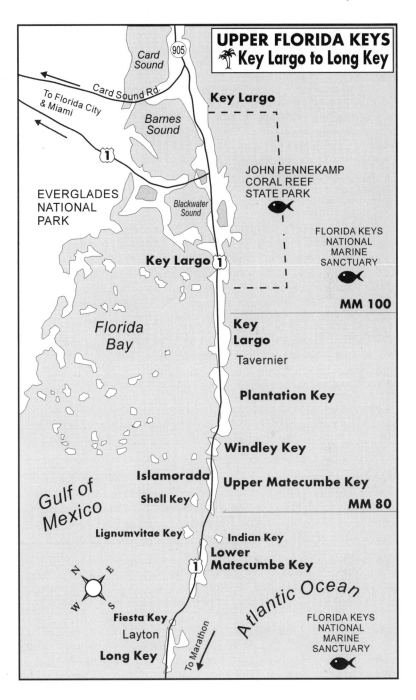

UPPER FLORIDA KEYS
Key Largo to Long Key

Card
Sound

905

Card Sound Rd.

To Florida City
& Miami

1

Barnes
Sound

Key Largo

EVERGLADES
NATIONAL
PARK

Blackwater
Sound

JOHN PENNEKAMP
CORAL REEF
STATE PARK

FLORIDA KEYS
NATIONAL
MARINE
SANCTUARY

Key Largo 1

MM 100

Florida
Bay

Key
Largo

Tavernier

Plantation Key

Windley Key

Islamorada

Upper Matecumbe Key

Shell Key

MM 80

Gulf of
Mexico

Lignumvitae Key

Indian Key

Lower
Matecumbe Key

1

Atlantic Ocean

FLORIDA KEYS
NATIONAL
MARINE
SANCTUARY

Fiesta Key

Layton

Long Key

To Marathon

**Best Western Suites**, MM 100, oceanside, rents canalside apartments with kitchens and screened patios. Boat docking. Group discounts and dive packages available. No pets. Write MM 100, 201 Ocean Drive, Key Largo FL 33037. ☎ 800-462-6079 or 305-451-5081.

**Holiday Inn Key Largo Resort**, MM 99.7, oceanside, is adjacent to a large marina with a boat ramp and docking for all size craft. The resort features 132 suites, restaurant, gift shop, freshwater pool with waterfall and fast access to diving and recreation facilities. It is also the home of the *African Queen*, used in the 1951 movie starring Humphrey Bogart and Katharine Hepburn. No pets. Moderate to deluxe. Write MM 100, 99701 Overseas Hwy, Key Largo FL 33037. ☎ US 800-THE-KEYS or 305-451-2121.

**Howard Johnson's Resort**, MM 102.3, bayside, features modern rooms, swimming in the pool or bay, sand beach, restaurant, balconies, beach bar, dock, dive and other packages. Color cable TV. Refrigerators and microwaves. Some small pets are allowed. Call first. Group rates available. Write MM 102, P.O. Box 1024, Key Largo FL 33037. ☎ 800-654-2000 or 305-451-1400. (Manatees are often spotted behind this resort in winter.)

**Island Bay Resort,** bayside at MM 92.5, features eight rooms with kitchen facilities, a boat dock and ramp, sandy beach and cable TV. No pets. Write P.O. Box 573, Tavernier FL. ☎ 305-852-4087 or 800-654-KEYS. Low.

**Kelly's Motel**, MM 104.5, sits in a sheltered cove. Boat dock and ramp. Dive trips. Sandy beach. Cooking facilities. Some pets. Write 104220 Overseas Hwy., Key Largo FL 33037. ☎ 305-451-1622 or 800-226-0415. Low to moderate.

**Keys Motel** is on the old Overseas Highway at MM 90.5 in Tavernier. Eighteen units. You can dock your boat at the adjacent deep water canal. No ramp. No pets. Kitchen facilities available. Low to moderate. Write 90611 Old Highway, Tavernier FL 33070. ☎ 305-852-2351 or 800-841-8902.

**Kona Kai Resort** at MM 97.8 is a nine-unit motel on the bay. Color cable TV, phones, fishing pier. Boat dock and ramp. No pets. Write 97802 Overseas Highway, Key Largo FL 33037. ☎ 305-852-7200 or 800-365-STAY. Low to moderate.

**Largo Lodge** at MM 101.5 is a charming bayside complex offering six apartments – all in a tropical garden setting. Guests must be at least 16 years old. Swimming. Small boat dock. Ramp. No pets. Write 101740 Overseas Highway, Key Largo FL 33037. ☎ 800-IN-THE-SUN (468-4378) or 305-451-0424. Moderate.

**Marriott Key Largo Bay Beach,** MM 103.8, bayside, features luxury accommodations, pool, beach, dive shop, watersports, two restaurants and three bars. ☎ 305-453-0000, 800-932-9332, fax 305-453-0093.

**Marina Del Mar Bayside,** MM99.5, offers 56 comfortable rooms, freshwater pool and dock. ☎ 800-242-5229, fax 305-451-9650.

**Marina Del Mar,** MM 100, oceanside, is a luxury dive resort on a deepwater marina in the heart of Key Largo. There are 130 rooms, suites and villas. Refrigerators in all rooms. The suites have complete kitchens. Rooms overlook the yacht basin or ocean. Dive shop on premises. Fishing charters. Meeting facilities. Waterfront restaurant and lounge. Write P.O. Box 1050, Key Largo FL 33037. ☎ 305-451-4107, US 800-451-3483, FL 800-253-3483, Canada 800-638-3483, fax 305-451-1891. Deluxe to ultra-deluxe.

**Ocean Pointe,** MM 92.5, oceanside, features one- and two-bedroom suites with jacuzzi tubs and fully equipped kitchens, private balconies, heated swimming pool with whirlpool spa, lighted tennis courts, marina with boat ramp and rental slips, waterfront café and lounge, white sandy suntan beach, watersports equipment. Money saving packages. No pets. Deluxe. ☎ 800-882-9464 or 305-3000, fax 305-853-3007.

**Popps Motel** on the bay at MM 95.5 has 10 units with cooking facilities, a small beach, boat dock and ramp. No pets. P.O. Box 43, Key Largo FL 33037. ☎ 305-852-5201, fax 852-5200. Moderate.

**Port Largo Villas,** MM 100, oceanside, in the heart of Key Largo, offers 24 two-bedroom, two-bath units with cable TV, jacuzzis, tennis court, sundeck. Boat dock and ramp. No pets. Write P.O. Box 1290, Key Largo FL 33037. ☎ 305-451-4847. Deluxe.

**Rock Reef Resort** at MM 98 offers clean, comfortable cottages and apartments on the bay with one, two, or three bedrooms. Playground, tropical gardens. Boat dock and ramp. Sandy beach. No pets. Write P.O. Box 73, Key Largo FL. ☎ 800-477-2343 or 305-852-2401. Low to moderate.

**Sheraton Key Largo,** MM 97, bayside, a splendid watersports resort, features 200 luxury rooms, two restaurants, lounge, nature trails, two pools with waterfall, pool bar and a large dock on the bay. Private beach. Caribbean Watersports at the beach shack. Meeting facilities. No pets. Write 97000 US Hwy 1, Key Largo FL 33037. ☎ 305-852-5553, worldwide 800-325-3535, FL 800-826-1006, fax 305-852-8669. Money saving packages available. Deluxe.

**Stone Ledge Resort,** MM 95.3, bayside, offers 19 conch-style motel rooms, sandy beach, boat dock. Ten of the units have kitchens. Refrigerators in all rooms. TV. No pets. Write P.O. Box 50, Key Largo FL 33037. ☎ 305-852-8114. Low to moderate.

**Tropic Vista Motel** at MM 90.5 sits on an oceanside canal. Dive shop on premises. Dock. Pets allowed in some rooms. Call first. Write P.O. Box 88, Tavernier FL 33070. ☎ 800-537-3253 or 305-852-8799. Low to moderate.

## KEY LARGO RV & TENT CAMPGROUNDS

**America Outdoors.** MM 97.5. Sandy beach, laundry, bathhouses. Boat dock, ramp and marina. RV sites. Pets allowed. Write 97450 Overseas Hwy., Key Largo FL 33037. ☎ 305-852-8054, fax 305-853-0509.

**Blue Lagoon Resort & Marina,** MM 99.6, bayside, rents and parks RVs. A couple of simple efficiencies for rent also. Parking is tight, but you are in the heart of Key Largo. Boat dock. Swimming. No pets. Write 99096 US Hwy 1, Key Largo FL 33037. ☎ 305-451-2908.

**Calusa Camp Resort.** MM 101.5, bayside waterfront RV park. Boat dock, ramp, marina, bait shop, camp store. Rentals. Pets allowed. Write 325 Calusa, Key Largo FL 33037. ☎ 800-457-2267 or 305-451-0232.

**Florida Keys RV Resort,** MM 106, oceanside, has cable on all sites, water, electric. Good Sam Park. Pets OK. Near dive shops. ☎ 800-252-6090, fax 451-5996.

**Key Largo Kampground.** MM 101.5. Oceanfront RV and tent sites, boat dock, ramp, laundry and bath house. Write P.O. Box 118-A, Key Largo FL 33037. ☎ 305-451-1431, US 800-KAMP-OUT.

**Point Laura Campground & Marina.** MM 112.5. Located six miles north of Key Largo's main area, this campground is best described as a sprawling marina with RV parking. It is somewhat isolated, but has fuel and a bath house. Good restaurant. Dockage. Ramp. Mosquitos. Pets allowed. Write 999 Morris Lane, Cross Key FL 33037. ☎ 305-451-0033.

## ISLAMORADA ACCOMMODATIONS
**Plantation Key to Long Key**

For a complete list of home rental agencies, contact the **Islamorada Chamber of Commerce**, P.O. Box 915, Islamorada FL 33036. ☎ 305-664-4503 or 1-800-FAB KEYS.

**Bud & Mary's Fishing Marina**, MM 79.8, oceanside, consists of six motel units. Private beach, 12 charter boats, 26 backcountry guides, rental boats, dive boat and party fishing. No pets. ☎ 305-664-2461.

**Breezy Palms Resort**, MM 80, on the ocean, offers one- , two-and three-room villas, beach cottages or studio efficiencies. All come with well-equipped kitchens, attractive furnishings. Maid service. Large swimming beach. Freshwater pool, boat harbor and ramp with a lighted dock for night fishing. No pets. Write P.O. Box 767, Islamorada FL 33036. Low to moderate. ☎ 305-664-2361, fax 305-664-2572.

**Caloosa Cove Resort**, MM 73.8, offers 30 deluxe oceanfront condos, one or two bedrooms with modern kitchens. Pool, lounge, restaurant, tennis, boat rentals, free breakfast and activities. Full service marina with dockage. No pets. Write 73801 US Hwy 1, Islamorada FL 33036. ☎ 305-664-8811, fax 305-664-8856.

**Cheeca Lodge** offers pampered seclusion, oceanside, at MM 82. Well described as being in "its own neighborhood," the resort offers guests a wealth of activities, including dive and snorkeling trips, a nine-hole golf course, sailing, fishing, tennis, parasailing, windsurfing, complete with a staff of expert instructors, captains or pros. Features include oversized guestrooms and villas, most with private balconies and paddle fans, a children's recreational camp, shops, gourmet dining, entertainment, palm-lined swimming/snorkeling beach, pool, 525-ft lighted fishing pier. Dockage and marina. Conference center. No pets. Deluxe. Write P.O. Box 527, Islamorada FL 33036. ☎ 305-664-4651 or 800-327-2888.

**Chesapeake of Whale Harbor**, adjacent to the Whale Harbor Restaurant and Islamorada docks, sprawls across six oceanfront acres at MM 83.5. The modern resort offers motel or efficiency units, a sand beach and deep water lagoon. Walk to fishing/charter boat docks. No pets. Write P.O. Box 909, Islamorada FL 33036. ☎ 800-338-3395 or 305-664-4662. Moderate to deluxe.

**El Capitan Resort**, MM 84, offers efficiencies for two to six people in the Holiday Isle complex. Oceanside lagoon and beach. Boat dockage. No pets. Write MM 84, Islamorada FL 33036. ☎ 305-664-2321, US 800-327-7070. Moderate to deluxe.

**Holiday Isle Resort** encompasses an entire beach club community with every imaginable watersport and activity. Guests choose from rooms, efficiencies or suites. The beach vibrates with reggae music. Vendors offer parasailing, fishing and diving charters, sailing, windsurfing, jet-skiing, inflatable-island rentals, sun lounges and dancing. Fast food stands offering barbecued dishes, pizza, ice cream, drinks and more are scattered about the grounds. There is a lovely rooftop restaurant and a unique chicken and ribs restaurant in the parking lot. Rooms are luxurious. The beach, open to everyone, is packed early during the high season. No pets. Write 84001 US Hwy 1, Islamorada FL. ☎ 305-664-2321, US 800-327-7070, fax 305-664-2703.

**Harbor Lights Motel,** oceanfront, is part of the Holiday Isle beach complex, offering efficiencies, rooms and cottages. Write 84001 US Hwy 1, Islamorada FL. ☎ 800-327-7070 or 305-664-3611, fax 305-664-2703.

**Howard Johnson Resort** oceanside at MM 84.5, adjacent to Holiday Isle, features a soft sand beach, restaurant. Guests wander back and forth to Holiday Isle beach. Boat dock and ramp. No pets. Write 84001 US Hwy 1, Islamorada FL 33036. ☎ US 800-654-2000 or 305-664-2711, fax 305-664-2703. Moderate to deluxe.

**La Jolla Resort,** MM 82.3, bayside, offers a quiet, tropical garden atmosphere. Kitchen units are comfortable. Boat dock and ramp. Small swimming beach, grills. Some pets, with restrictions. Call first. Write Box 51, Islamorada FL 33036. ☎ 305-664-9213. Low to moderate.

**Lime Tree Bay Resort,** at MM 68.5, is an older motel, but comfortable, with beautiful grounds. Kitchen units available. There is a restaurant, tennis court, boat dock and beach with a freshwater pool. No pets. Write P.O. Box 839, Long Key FL 33001. ☎ 305-664-4740 or 800-723-4519. Low to moderate.

**Ocean 80 Inc.,** MM 80.5, oceanside, features luxury efficiencies or suites with fully-equipped kitchens. Tiki bar, restaurant, tennis, pool and jet-ski rentals. Adjacent to full-service marina. Boat dock. No pets. P.O. Box 949, Islamorada FL 33036. Deluxe. ☎ 305-664-4411, US 800-367-9050.

**Plantation Yacht Harbor Resort,** MM 87, bayside, features tennis courts, private beach, jet-skis and a huge marina with protected docking for large and small craft. A dive shop and lovely restaurant overlook the bay. No pets. Write 87000 US Hwy 1, Plantation Key, Islamorada FL 33036. ☎ 305-852-2381, fax 852-2381-555. Moderate to deluxe.

**Ragged Edge,** MM 86.5, oceanside, offers one- and two-bedroom air-conditioned suites and motel rooms, color TV, laundry room, guest boat harbor, marina dockage, ramps, deep water channel, fishing pier. ☎ 305-852-5389.

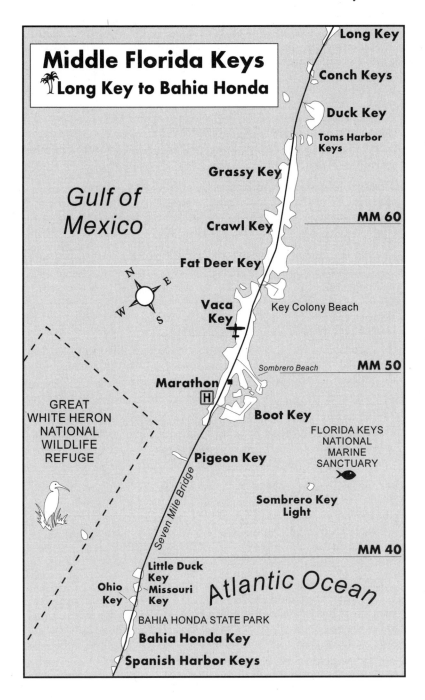

# Middle Florida Keys
## Long Key to Bahia Honda

Long Key

Conch Keys

Duck Key

Toms Harbor Keys

Grassy Key

*Gulf of Mexico*

Crawl Key

MM 60

Fat Deer Key

N
E
W
S

Vaca Key

Key Colony Beach

Sombrero Beach

MM 50

Marathon
H

Boot Key

GREAT WHITE HERON NATIONAL WILDLIFE REFUGE

FLORIDA KEYS NATIONAL MARINE SANCTUARY

Pigeon Key

Sombrero Key Light

Seven Mile Bridge

MM 40

Little Duck Key

Ohio Key

Missouri Key

*Atlantic Ocean*

BAHIA HONDA STATE PARK

Bahia Honda Key

Spanish Harbor Keys

**Tropical Reef Resort**, MM 85, oceanside, offers three fresh-water pools (one child-sized), picnic beach with tiki huts and floating breakfast café, marina and boat rentals. No pets. Write 849 US 1, Islamorada FL 33036. ☎ 305-664-8881 or 800-887-3373, fax 305-664-4891. Low to deluxe.

## ISLAMORADA CAMPGROUNDS

**Fiesta Key KOA**, MM 70, bayside, sits on a 28-acre tropical island surrounded by warm Gulf waters. 350 sites. Marina, docks and ramp. ☎ 305-664-4922.

**Long Key State Recreation Area**, MM 66, bayside, features two nature trails, bike and canoe rental, picnic area, observation tower, guided walks. No pets. ☎ 305-664-4815.

**Outdoor Resorts**, MM 66, bayside, has 30 RV sites with full hook-ups, tennis, shuffleboard, dock, ramp and marina. Pets OK. ☎ 305-664-4860.

## MARATHON ACCOMMODATIONS

For a complete list of rental units, condos and villas contact the **Greater Marathon Chamber of Commerce**, 12222 Overseas Hwy, Marathon FL 33050. ☎ 305-743-5417 or 800-842-9580.

**Banana Bay Resort & Marina**, MM 49.5, bayside, features 60 rooms, tennis, charter fishing and diving, huge pool and conference room. Sandy beach and snorkeling area. Boat ramp and dock. No pets. Write 4590 US Hwy 1, Marathon FL 33050. ☎ 800-BANANA-1 or 305-743-3500. Moderate to deluxe.

**Buccaneer Resort**, MM 48.5, bayside, has 76 units, beach, café, tennis, boat dock and charters. Dive shop on premises. Some kitchen units. Waterfront restaurant and tiki bar, sandy beach, fishing docks, wave runners. Write 2600 Overseas Hwy, Marathon FL 33050. ☎ US 800-237-3329 or 305-743-9071. Economy cottages and luxury villas. Low to moderate.

**Conch Key Cottages**, MM 62.3, oceanside, are situated on a secluded, private island which up until recently could only be reached by boat. New owners have built a landfill roadway so you can drive the short distance from US 1. Rustic 50s-style wooden cottages have screened-in porches and huge ceiling fans. Pool. All air-conditioned with cable TV, hammock and barbecue. Coin washer and dryers on premises. Boat dock and ramp. Well behaved pets are welcome. Call first. Write Box 424, Marathon FL 33050. ☎ 800-330-1577 or 305-289-1377. Moderate to deluxe.

**Holiday Inn of Marathon**, MM 54, oceanside, has 134 rooms, restaurant, and bar. Abyss Dives shop on property. Boat ramp and marina. Pets OK. Write 13201 US Hwy 1, Marathon FL 33050. ☎ 800-224-5053, 800-HOLIDAY or 305-289-0222. For dive/hotel packages, 800-457-0134. Moderate.

**Faro Blanco Marine Resort**, MM 48, spreads over two shores with the most diverse selection of facilities on the Atlantic and the Gulf. Choose from houseboat suites, condos, garden cottages, or an apartment in the Faro Blanco lighthouse for a special treat.There is a full-service marina if you are arriving by yacht and wish to tie up for a stay. Dockmaster stands by on VHF Channel 16. Convenient to fine restaurants and diving. Pets allowed in the houseboats and cottages, but not the condos. Children under 18 not allowed in the condos. Write 1996 US Hwy 1, Marathon FL 33050. ☎ 800-759-3276. Moderate to deluxe.

**Hawks Cay Resort and Marina** offers 177 spacious rooms and suites. Heated pool, saltwater lagoon with sandy beach, 18-hole golf course nearby, marine mammal training center featuring dolphin shows for guests. Charter fishing and diving boats leave from the marina. Protected boat slips for large and small craft. No pets. Write MM 61, Duck Key FL 33050. ☎ 305-743-7000, FL 800-432-2242, fax 305-743-5215. Ultra-deluxe.

**Howard Johnson Resort**, MM 54, bayside, has a private beach, dive shop, dock and marina, restaurant. Pets OK. Write 13351 US Hwy 1, Marathon FL 33050. ☎ 800-654-2000 or 305-743-8550, fax 305-743-8550. Moderate.

**Kingsail Resort Motel**, MM 50. Bayside accommodations range from modern, attractive rooms to well-equipped efficiencies and one-bedroom apartments. There is a boat ramp, dock, grocer, pool, shaded tiki. No pets. Fishing and diving charters. Write P.O. Box 986, Marathon FL 33050. ☎ 305-743-5246, FL 800-423-7474, fax 305-743-8896. Low to moderate.

**Ocean Beach Club**, 3551 E. Ocean Dr. East, Key Colony Beach, features 38 guest rooms, sandy white beach, hot tub and fishing pier. No pets. ☎ 305-289-0525 or 800-321-7213, fax 305-289-9703.

**Rainbow Bend Fishing Resort**, oceanside at MM 58, offers free use of a motorboat or sailboat with every room plus complimentary breakfast daily. There is a wide sandy beach, pool, fishing pier, tackle shop. Dive and fishing charters. Rooms and efficiencies. Café. Pets OK. Write P.O. Box 2447, Grassy Key FL 33050. ☎ 305-289-1505, fax 305-743-4257.

**Sombrero Resort,** 19 Sombrero Blvd. Centrally located in the Middle Keys, the all-suite resort is good for groups. Restaurant, lounge, tiki bar, pool, sauna, four lighted tennis courts, marina, beach and golf nearby. Moderate to deluxe. ☎ 800-433-8660, fax 305-743-2250.

The **Seahorse Motel,** at MM 51, bayside, offers protected dock space, a playground, pool, barbecue patio, quiet rooms and efficiencies. Write 7196 US Hwy 1, Marathon FL 33050. Low. ☎ 305-743-6571 or 800-874-1115, fax 305-743-0775.

Additional and varied Marathon accommodations are offered through **AA Accommodation Center, Inc.,** ☎ 800-732-2006 or 305-296-7707.

## BIG PINE KEY ACCOMMODATIONS

Big Pine is between Marathon and Key West. A 20-minute drive will get you to either. For a complete list of Lower Keys accommodations, call, write or visit: **Lower Keys Chamber of Commerce,** PO Box 430511, Big Pine Key FL 33043. ☎ 800-872-3722 or 305-872-2411.

**Big Pine Resort Motel,** located at MM 30.5, bayside, offers the serenity of an out island with nearby proximity to Looe Key Marine Sanctuary. The motel has 32 large and comfortable rooms, efficiencies and apartments. Adjacent restaurant. No pets. Rt 5, Box 796, Big Pine Key FL 33043. ☎ 305-872-9090.

**Dolphin Marina Resort,** MM28.5, oceanside, is the closest marina to Looe Key Marine Sanctuary. Twelve simple motel rooms. No pets. Snorkel and sunset cruises daily. ☎ 800-942-5397 or 305-872-2685. Moderate.

**Parmer's Place Resort Motel,** MM 28.5, bayside, features 38 furnished efficiencies and one handicapped unit. Quiet. No pets. ☎ 305-872-2157, fax 305-872-2014. Low.

## LITTLE TORCH KEY ACCOMMODATIONS

**Little Palm Island.** Located on an out island, this deluxe resort offers all recreational facilities: day sailers, windsurfers, fishing gear, snorkel gear, canoes and bicycles. Suites include private balcony, ceiling fans, air conditioning, coffee maker, refrigerator, wet bar and whirlpool. Launch transfers to the island are provided. No TV or phones. Write to Overseas Highway 1, MM 28.5, Route 4, Box 1036, Little Torch Key FL 33042. ☎ 1-800 GET LOST (343-8567) or 305-872-2524.

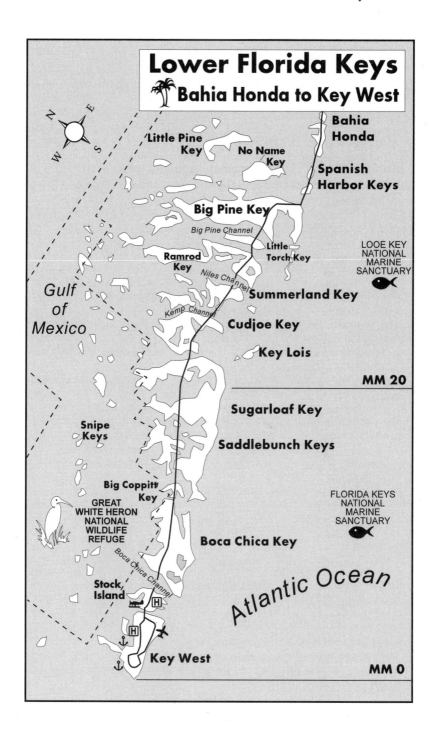

Lower Florida Keys
Bahia Honda to Key West

Little Pine Key

No Name Key

Bahia Honda

Spanish Harbor Keys

Big Pine Key

Big Pine Channel

Little Torch Key

LOOE KEY NATIONAL MARINE SANCTUARY

Ramrod Key

Niles Channel

Summerland Key

Gulf of Mexico

Kemp Channel

Cudjoe Key

Key Lois

MM 20

Sugarloaf Key

Snipe Keys

Saddlebunch Keys

Big Coppitt Key

GREAT WHITE HERON NATIONAL WILDLIFE REFUGE

FLORIDA KEYS NATIONAL MARINE SANCTUARY

Boca Chica Key

Boca Chica Channel

Atlantic Ocean

Stock Island

Key West

MM 0

## SUGARLOAF KEY ACCOMMODATIONS

**Sugarloaf Lodge**, at MM 17, bayside, is a complete resort with miniature golf, airstrip, restaurant, boat rentals, fishing charters, tennis, pool and marina. Moderate. PO Box 148, Sugarloaf Key FL 33044. ☎ 305-745-3211. Low.

## LOWER KEYS CAMPGROUNDS

**Sugarloaf Key KOA**, MM20, oceanside, offers 184 sites on 14 acres, full-service marina with canoe and boat rentals, game room, pool, hot tub, sandy beach, restaurant, laundry facilities and full-service store. ☎ 305-745-3549. Write to PO Box 469, Summerland Key FL 33044.

## KEY WEST ACCOMMODATIONS

Key West has three main resort areas – Old Town, the center of activity and where you'll find the island's most posh, oceanfront resort complexes, South Roosevelt Blvd., which runs along the south shore parallel to the Atlantic Ocean, and North Roosevelt Blvd., the commercial strip packed with fast food joints and strip malls that runs along the island's northern, Gulf shores. Because the island is just two miles wide and four miles long, no matter where you stay, you can travel to any point within a matter of minutes.

For a complete list of Key West accommodations, including guest houses, condominiums and apartments and vacation homes, contact the **Greater Key West Chamber of Commerce**, Mallory Square, 402 Wall St., Key West FL 33040. ☎ 800-LAST KEY or 305-294-2587.

**Atlantic Shores Motel**, 510 South St. Centrally located 72-room motel across from the ocean, near most attractions. Fishing pier, pool, some kitchen units. Moderate. ☎ 800-874-6730 or 305-296-2491.

**Best Western Hibiscus Motel**, 1313 Simonton St., offers 61 rooms in a tropical park-like setting. Two queen beds and refrigerator in each room, heated pool. Some kitchen units. No pets. ☎ 305-296-6711.

**Best Western Key Ambassador Resort Inn**, 3755 S. Roosevelt Blvd. Airport pick-up. Pool, balconies, in-room fridge. Close to beach. 101 units. ☎ 305-296-3500, US 1-800-432-4315. Deluxe.

**Blue Lagoon**, 3101 N. Roosevelt Blvd. This 72-room, older Gulf-front motel offers tropical atmosphere, cable TV, restaurant and bar. Low to moderate. ☎ 305-296-1043, fax 305-296-6499.

**Comfort Inn**, 3824 N. Roosevelt Blvd. Features 100 guest rooms. Family plans, Olympic pool. Low to moderate. ☎ 305-294-3773.

**Curry Mansion Inn**, 511 Caroline St. Nestled alongside the original 1899 Curry Mansion, the Inn offers 15 elegant romantic rooms, each opening onto a sparkling pool and surrounded by the lush foliage of the Curry Estate. Private baths and phones, wet bars, air conditioning, ceiling fans and TV. Deluxe. ☎ 305-294-5349.

**Days Inn Key West**, 3852 N. Roosevelt Blvd. Offers 134 rooms and suites, some with kitchens. Gift shop, restaurant, pool. Weekly/monthly rates available. This motel is on the highway at the beginning of Key West as you enter from Stock Island. Pets welcome. Low to moderate rates. ☎ 800-325-2525 or 305-294-3742.

**Econo Lodge Resort of Key West**, 3820 N. Roosevelt Blvd. This 134-room family resort features tiki bar, off-street parking, 24-hr. Dennys. Low to deluxe. No pets. ☎ 800-999-7277 or 305-294-5511.

**Fairfield Inn by Marriot**, 2400 N. Roosevelt Blvd., Key West FL 33040. One hundred rooms, heated pool, tiki bar, cable TV, free local calls. Closest hotel to the wharf. Some kitchen units. No pets. Handicapped accessible. ☎ US 800-228-2800 or 305-296-5700. Moderate to deluxe.

**Holiday Inn La Concha Hotel**, 430 Duval St., Key West FL 33040. This historic hotel towers over the center of Old Town. Renovated in 1986, this charming resort features 160 elegant rooms, a restaurant, fitness room, whirlpool spa, shops and the best view of the city from the rooftop lounge. Walk to all attractions, fishing and sightseeing. Meetings and receptions for up to 200 people. ☎ 800-745-2191 or 305-296-2991, fax 305-294-3283. Handicapped accessible. Deluxe.

**Holiday Inn Beachside**, 1111 N. Roosevelt Blvd., Key West FL 33030. Located directly on the Gulf of Mexico, this resort offers 222 lovely rooms, 79 having water views. Amenities include large freshwater pool, whirlpool, on site watersports and dive trips, gift shop, full-service restaurant and bar, two lighted tennis courts and full catering facilities. Soft sand beach, wave runners. Oceanfront and poolside rooms. Diving and snorkeling tours. Convenient to both sides of the island and Stock Island. Deluxe. No pets. ☎ 800-HOLIDAY or 305-294-2571.

**Hampton Inn**, 2801 N. Roosevelt Blvd., Key West FL 33040. Located on the Gulf, Hampton Inn features 157 units, island decor, freshwater pool, cable TV, Showtime, heated jacuzzi, tiki bar, sundeck. Handicapped accessible. Some pets OK. ☎ 305-294-2917, US 1-800-HAMPTON. Deluxe.

**Howard Johnson Resort**, 3031 N. Roosevelt Blvd., Key West FL 33040. Adjacent to recreation center and Key Plaza shopping center. Pool, restaurant. ☎ 800-942-0913 or 305-296-6595, fax 296-8351.

**Hyatt Key West Resort and Marina**, 601 Front St, Key West FL 33040. Oceanfront, this stunning 120-room landmark resort sits two short blocks from Duval and the heart of Old Town. Pool, three fine restaurants, private sandy beach and marina. ☎ US 800-233-1234 or 305-296-9900. Deluxe.

**Key Wester Resort**, 3675 S. Roosevelt Blvd. Sprawled across nine acres on the Atlantic, the 100-room resort features an Olympic pool, tiki bar and café at poolside, two tennis courts. One half-mile to beach, 2½ miles to town. No pets. Moderate to deluxe. ☎ 800-477-8888.

**The Marquesa Hotel**, 600 Fleming St. A small very grand hotel in a landmark 1884 house. Located in the heart of Old Town, the hotel offers 15 luxurious rooms, private baths, heated pool. Restaurant. ☎ 800-869-4631 or 305-292-1919, fax 294-2121.

**Marriott's Casa Marina Resort**, 1500 Reynolds St. Billed as the island's largest oceanfront resort, featuring 314 rooms, tennis, bicycles, water sports, private beach, two pools, whirlpool and sauna. Complete health club on premises. Lovely mahogany pool-bar with barbecue services. Lounge. Handicapped accessible. Deluxe. ☎ US 1-800-288-9290, FL 1-800-235-4837 or 305-296-3535.

**Marriot Reach Resort**, 1435 Simonton St. Elegant resort located on a natural sand beach. Features 149 rooms (80 suites), each with a veranda, most with ocean view, ceiling fans, wet bar, two restaurants, oceanside dining, watersports, food store, library, five bars, entertainment. Health center, lap pool. Handicapped accessible. No pets. Deluxe. ☎ US 1-800-874-4118 or 305-296-5000.

**Ocean Key House Suite Resort & Marina**, on Mallory Square at Zero Duval St., offers deluxe suites on the Gulf of Mexico. Fully equipped kitchens, jacuzzi. Private balcony with water and sunset views. VCR and movie rentals. No pets. ☎ US 800-328-9815, FL 800-231-9864, fax 305-292-7685.

**Old Town Resorts, Inc.** at 1319 Duval St. in Old Town includes the southernmost motel in the US, the South Beach Oceanfront Motel, and the La Mer Hotel. Offers three pools, jacuzzi, tiki bar, sunning pier on the Atlantic, gift shop, dive shop, concierge. Walking distance to beach, shops, nightlife and dining. No pets. Moderate to deluxe. ☎ 305-296-6577, FL 1-800-354-4455, fax 294-8272.

**Pegasus International Motel**, 501 Southard St., Key West FL 33040. Art Deco hotel. Old world service in Old Town at reasonable rates. 23 units. No pets. TV, private bath, air conditioning. Low to moderate. ☎ 800-397-8148 or 305-294-9323, fax 294-4741.

**Pelican Landing Resort & Marina**, 915 Eisenhower Dr. Luxury suites sleep two to eight people. No pets. Full kitchens, heated pool, barbecue grills, cable TV, docks, fish cleaning station, barbecue grill, HBO. Two penthouses with jacuzzi. ☎ 800-527-8108 or 305-296-7583. Low to deluxe.

**Pier House Hotel**, One Duval St. In the heart of Old Town Key West. Offers 142 eclectic, romantic guest rooms and suites with private terraces. Private beach, full-service spa, heated pool. Five restaurants, five bars, beachside entertainment. No pets. Deluxe. ☎ US 800-327-8340 or 305-296-4600, fax 305-296-7568.

**Quality Inn Resort**, 3850 N. Roosevelt Blvd. Typical large chain features include pool, kitchen units, free coffee makers and coffee in each room. Pool, free HBO. Low to deluxe. ☎ 800-553-5024 or 305-294-6681, fax 305-294-5618.

**Ramada Inn**, 3420 N. Roosevelt Blvd. On the commercial strip across highway from the Gulf of Mexico. Air conditioned. Color TV, pool, tennis. Pets welcome. Handicapped accessible. ☎ 800-330-5541 or 305-294-5541. Low to deluxe.

**Santa Maria Motel**, 1401 Simonton St. Simple motel close to Old Town. Olympic freshwater pool. Low to moderate. ☎ 800-821-KEYS or 305-296-5678, fax 294-0010.

**Sheraton Suites Key West**, 2001 S. Roosevelt Blvd. A 180-suite hotel just a quarter-mile from Key West Airport. All suites have a fridge, microwave, remote TV, free breakfast. Large pool, complimentary shuttle to and from Key West Airport and Old Town. Large meeting rooms. ☎ 305-292-9800, fax 294-6009.

**Southernmost Motel in the USA**, 1319 Duval. Features two pools, jacuzzi, tiki bar poolside, walking distance to shops, nightlife, attractions, across from beach pier on ocean. ☎ 800-354-4455 or 305-296-6577.

## KEY WEST CAMPGROUNDS

**Boyd's Campground,** Maloney Ave., Stock Island FL 33040. Southernmost campground in the US, on the Atlantic Ocean. Features all watersports, showers restrooms, laundry, store, ice, city bus, telephone, dump station, bottle gas, electric, water, sewer hookups. Twenty boat slips and launching ramps. Pets OK. Pool. MC/Visa. ☎ 305-294-1465.

**Jabour's Trailer Court,** 223 Elizabeth, St., Key West FL 33040. Waterfront campground in Old Town Key West. Walking distance to everything. Tents and RVs welcome. Efficiencies. ☎ 305-294-5723.

**Leo's Campground & RV Park,** 5236 Suncrest Rd., Stock Island FL 33040. Features 36 shady sites. Electric hookups, hot and cold showers, laundry, dump station. Security seven days a week. Barbecues. ☎ 296-5260.

# Everglades National Park

Please note that, although the park is open year round, the recreational services are open from mid-November to mid-April.

**Flamingo Lodge, Marina & Outpost Resort** is the only lodging inside Everglades National Park. Get there by taking Florida Turnpike or Route 1 to Florida City, then follow signs to Everglades National Park and Flamingo. It takes about 45 minutes to drive the 38-mile distance from the main entrance to Flamingo. Rooms are air-conditioned, modern and comfortable. Freshwater pool. Absolutely no pets. Full service from November 1 through April 30. Moderate. ☎ 305-253-2241 or 941-695-3101. Write to P.O. Box 428, Flamingo FL 33030.

For the northwestern or Ten Thousand Islands region, contact **Everglades Area Chamber of Commerce,** P.O. Box 130, Everglades City FL 33929, ☎ 914-695-3941.

## CAMPING

Camping in Everglades National Park is on a first-come, first-served basis. Long Pine Key has 108 sites, Flamingo has 235 drive-in sites and 60 walk-in sites for tents. Fees are $8 per night for the regular sites, $4 per night for the Flamingo walk-in sites. Group campsites are $10 per night at both locations (maximum 15 people) and may be reserved in advance. Camping is restricted to 14 days per visit and a total of 30 days per year. Arrive early to obtain a site. Checkout time is 10 am. There are no water or electrical hookups.

Restrooms, drinking water and sanitary dump stations are at both campgrounds; cold water showers at Flamingo only. Limited groceries and camping supplies may be purchased at the Flamingo Marina Store. Long Pine Key has no camp store and all supplies must be obtained in Homestead. Pets are allowed at the campgrounds.

## BACKCOUNTRY CAMPING

Backcountry Use Permits are required for all overnight use of the backcountry (except on board boats) and may be obtained at Flamingo and Everglades City ranger stations. Most sites are chickees – elevated wooden platforms with a roof and chemical toilet – accessible only by boat. Length of stay and number of people are restricted. Pets are not allowed on developed trails or in the backcounry.

# Northern Everglades

## TEN THOUSAND ISLAND REGION

This jungle-like area of mangrove islands offers fishermen and canoe campers an untouched wilderness experience. Sightseeing and airboat excursions featuring alligator- , manatee- , and frog-watching rank high in popularity.

## EVERGLADES CITY

**Everglades' Rod and Gun Resort Lodge.** Motel accommodations, heated pool, waterfront restaurant, lounge and full-service marina. No pets. Write to P.O. Box 190, Everglades City FL 33929. ☎ 941-695-2101.

**Port of the Islands Resort** offers deluxe sportsman accommodations, an RV park, a trap and skeet range, pool, tennis and sightseeing cruises. No pets. ☎ US 1-800-237-4173 or 914-394-3101.

**Sportsman's Club** has motel rooms and efficiencies. Some small, quiet pets allowed. Call first. Write P.O. Box 399 (318 Mamie St), Chokoloskee FL 33925. ☎ 941-695-4224.

## CAMPING

**Outdoor Resorts** is an RV campground well-suited for boaters. Forty-eight of the 283 sites have dockage on the bay. Additional dockage for 65 boats. All sites are landscaped with paved drives and patios. Fully equipped marina with boat ramp, bait shop, boat rental, three pools, spa with saunas, tennis. Motel. Pets are allowed in the campground, but not in the motel. Write P.O. Box 429, Chokoloskee FL 33925. ☎ 941-695-2881.

**Glades Haven** at the Everglades City entrance to Everglades National Park offers tent and RV sites. The campground features ocean access, dockage, boat ramp, bath, showers and club house. Home of North American Canoe Tours. Write 800 S.E. Copeland Ave., Everglades City FL 33929. ☎ 941-695-2746.

# Index